D1606295

Princess Patricia's Canadian Light Infantry

Also by Jeffery Williams
BYNG OF VIMY – General and Governor-General

Princess Patricia's Canadian Light Infantry

by Jeffery Williams

Leo Cooper
in association with
Secker & Warburg

First published in Great Britain
by Leo Cooper in 1972
Revised Second Edition published in 1985
by Leo Cooper in association with
Martin Secker & Warburg Limited,
54 Poland Street, London W1V 3DF

Copyright © Jeffery Williams 1972, 1985

ISBN 0-436-57111-0

Printed and bound in Great Britain at
The Camelot Press Ltd., Southampton

To the Memory
of
Francis Farquhar
and
Alexander Hamilton Gault

Contents

Illustrations

Foreword

THE author was fortunate that two such eminent writers as Ralph Hodder-Williams and Lieutenant-Colonel G. R. Stevens served in Princess Patricia's Canadian Light Infantry in the First World War. The former wrote the history of the Regiment in that conflict and the latter continued the story until 1957. Another Patricia, Lieutenant-Colonel G. W. L. Nicholson, produced the official history of the Canadian Army in Italy 1943–45 and a fourth, Lieutenant-Colonel Herbert Fairlie Wood, wrote the history of the Canadians in Korea. These works by his brother officers have been the author's most important sources.

Many members of the Regiment have helped him. He is especially grateful to the late Mrs Hamilton Gault for commenting on the draft of the first edition and for providing photographs from the Founder's collection, and to Mrs H. F. Wood, Maj-Gen C. B. Ware, Brig-Gen L. A. Bourgeois, Brig-Gen C. B. Snider, Lt-Col W. E. J. Hutchinson, Major H. F. Elliott and Captain Vernon Cole for their valuable help and advice.

Writing the original version of the book was his wife's idea and it was she who typed and re-typed the drafts. She has done so once more with this edition. He owes her a particular debt.

In 1984 the author was invited by the Regiment to bring the original version up to date. It now reflects the first seventy years of the history of the Patricias and is published on the authority of the Regimental Executive Committee, Princess Patricia's Canadian Light Infantry, Calgary, Alberta, Canada – 1984.

Chapter I
The Originals

D URING July and the first hot days of August, 1914, Canadians were an audience to the opening of a fascinating stylized drama. There was a quality of unreality about the diplomatic moves reported from Europe. And yet there was an inevitability – a sense that all was preordained. As assassination was followed by ultimatum, by affirmation of treaty obligation, by mobilization, so it was realized that the time had come for the long-awaited war with Germany.

No one expected Canada to take a part in the prologue. Yet there was no doubt of her coming involvement. 'When Britain is at war, Canada is at war'. Prime Minister Sir Wilfrid Laurier's statement in 1910 was promptly echoed by the Leader of the Opposition. In 1912, Sam Hughes, the Minister of Militia and Defence had proclaimed that Germany needed to be taught the lesson that Canada and the other Dominions were behind the Mother Country.

In Ottawa, at the end of July, the Government worried over the mobilization plans of the Militia. Compared to the pace of events across the Atlantic, they seemed too deliberate, too pedestrian. The most respected authorities on the subject held that a war between the major powers in Europe would be over in six months or less. (Only Lord Kitchener seems to have held a more realistic view.) There was a serious possibility that the war would end before Canadian troops could reach the field.

It was this sense of urgency which was later to speed the training of Canadian Militiamen and get them to France before the first of the British Territorial divisions arrived.

Others, too, felt the urgency of the situation. The chances seemed better than even that most Canadians would be spectators, on the sidelines of one of the most exciting events in history. How lucky the British were to be so close to the scene! The first two days of August fell at a weekend and many had used the time away from work to decide what they should do when war came. On Monday, the 3rd, one of them climbed onto the early morning train from Montreal to Ottawa. He had a proposal to discuss with Sam Hughes.

At nineteen years of age, Andrew Hamilton Gault had been an officer of the 2nd Canadian Mounted Rifles in South Africa and now, at 33, was a captain of the Royal Highlanders of Canada, a Montreal militia regiment. He had been impressed by the performance of the irregular cavalry of the Dominions in that unimaginative war with the Boers. One of those regiments would be doubly effective operating against the stereotyped tactics of the continental cavalry.

In his own eyes, Hamilton Gault was a typical officer of the Militia. He belonged to it because he believed that every gentleman had a military obligation to his country and he enjoyed the society of men who held that view. He did not consider that the commitment of an officer was limited to his person but extended to his purse and possessions as well. Few Militia Officers ever drew the small amount of pay the government provided but assigned it to their units to pay for essentials. No boots were issued to the militia and it was not unusual for an officer to buy them for men who could not afford them. The good officer should do anything he could for his men, for his regiment, for his country. Gault counted himself fortunate in being wealthy because it meant that he could do more. He now was prepared to pay for raising a regiment and he would volunteer to serve in it himself.

He had already drawn up a tentative list of officers, most being members of the Militia. Those whom he had approached were enthusiastic about joining if their own regiments were not mobilized. The regimental history tells of one who was eager to be a company commander but was required instead for the First Canadian Contingent and became a brigadier-general before the end of September.

When Gault arrived at his office, Col Sam Hughes, the Minister of Militia and Defence was involved in a conference which was considering what Canada should do about the developing situation in Europe. They met during a short break in the proceedings. Gault stated his proposal briefly. If war was declared, he would raise and equip a mounted unit at his own expense to be placed at the disposal of the Imperial authorities. The impetuous Hughes found the project attractive and said that the Government would certainly consider it. He thought, though, that infantry would be of more general use than cavalry and would be more urgently required. Gault readily agreed to modify his plan.

Before returning to Montreal, he met Lt-Col Francis Farquhar, Military Secretary to the Duke of Connaught, Governor General of Canada, who had already learned of the offer from Hughes. This highly competent professional soldier offered to help in any way that he could.

War was declared the next day and Farquhar sent a wire to Gault asking him to come at Ottawa at once. Farquhar was well aware of the theory of the short war. Unlike the man in the street who was worried that Canadians might not be in on the kill, he was more concerned with a little-known corollary – that the country which concentrated its power with the greatest speed would be the victor.

On the evening of 5 August, Col Farquhar told Gault that it looked very much as if his proposal would be accepted by the Canadian Government. It was also apparent that Canada would raise a considerable force from the Militia and that that source of officers and men would be denied to the new unit. There were thousands of ex-regular soldiers and veterans of the Boer War in Canada. If the new regiment were to recruit them, only a minimum of training would be needed. They could be in the field in a few weeks. The following is a copy of Farquhar's plan.

THE PROJECT

1. The raising of two double companies, organized as a self-contained half battalion, strength all ranks 500 men.

2. Recruiting.

   The scheme of recruiting not in any degree to clash with the Militia, my object being to make use of the many men now in Canada who have seen service and who are not at present enlisted in any unit. These men should shake down quickly.

3. Sources of Recruiting.
   (a) Police forces such as the CPR, Toronto and Winnipeg police, etc.
   (b) Various veterans' societies or associations.
   (c) Advertisement in papers.

4. Qualifications.
   (a) Having seen active service (?)
   (b) Age 35 or less.
   (c) Physically fit.
   (d) Ex-regular soldiers to have at least a 'fair' character certificate. Other recruits to have an analogous 'character'.
   (e) Any man drawn from the Militia to produce written permission to enlist from the O.C. his Militia Battalion.

That night, an outline plan was made for the formation of the unit. Farquhar would command and Gault would be the senior major. They would ask Her Royal Highness, the Princess Patricia of Connaught to lend her name to the Regiment. The Duke of Connaught would have to be asked for permission to associate his daughter with the project and, of course, to release Farquhar from his duties as Military Secretary. Gault noted 'Princess Patricia's Own Canadian Light Infantry' as a possible title.

Next day, the plan was agreed by the Governor General, the Princess and the Canadian Government. On 8 August, the British Government wired their approval and an agreement was signed by the Minister of Militia and Defence and Major Hamilton Gault.

The first recruiting posters for the Patricia's appeared on 11 August in Montreal, Toronto, Ottawa, Winnipeg, Calgary and Edmonton. Nine days later, after interviewing nearly 3,000

1. *Princess Patricia of Connaught – Colonel-in-Chief 1914–74.*

2. *Major A. Hamilton Gault, the Founder.*

3. *The Regiment at Lévis, Quebec. September, 1914.*

4. *Lt-Col F. D. Farquhar, DSO, and his adjutant, Capt H. C. Buller with the Ric-a-dam-doo.*

5. *Lt W. G. Colquhoun, Battalion Scout Officer, "Shelley Farm," February, 1915.*

6. *The Machine Gun Section, Salisbury Plain, 1914. Major Hamilton Gault is on the left.*

7. *The Adjutant, Capt. L. V. Drummond-Hay, congratulates Sgt G. H. Mullin, MM, on being awarded the Victoria Cross.*

8. *Major C. J. T. Stewart, DSO with Lt-Col Agar Adamson, DSO, France, 1917*

9. *Ceremonial parade, somewhere in France, 1918. Lt-Col C. J. T. Stewart commanding, rides behind the Ric-a-dam-doo.*

10. *The Originals at Frezenberg, from the painting by W. B. Wollen, RI*

applicants and selecting 1,098, Col Farquhar declared mobilization complete. In their eagerness to join, a race had developed among prospective recruits. One group is said to have high-jacked a train to take them to Ottawa and stories are legion of men driving to the nearest station, hitching their horses to a rail and boarding the first train to the East. On 19 August, the battalion had on its strength former members of every British and Canadian regular regiment but one (which that was is not recorded). The Royal Navy and the Marines were represented. Nearly all had been born in Britain and had come to Canada after military service.

At the first church parade after mobilization, it was apparent that something was different about this new regiment. It bore the title of Light Infantry. (The Founder, as Hamilton Gault is now known, had thought of 'Light Horse' for the name of the cavalry unit he had intended to raise because there was an 'irregular tang' about it. He liked 'Light Infantry' for the same reason). Their drill reminded many of the Guards, but then Francis Farquhar and several of his NCO's had come from the Brigade, and they had more pressing things to do than to learn a new drill manual. After Princess Patricia had presented them with a colour which she herself had designed and made, they marched past to *Blue Bonnets Over the Border* played by their pipe band which wore the Hunting Stewart tartan. The Pipe Major had arrived with his band from Edmonton and had told the Commanding Officer that they had come to play the Regiment to France and back.

The Colour which the Princess presented was not an official 'Regimental Colour', its design approved by the College of Heralds, but rather was intended simply to mark headquarters of the Battalion in the field. But it had much more significance than a mere camp colour to the Regiment. That parade in Lansdowne Park in Ottawa was no routine affair for the men who had come to serve again. Soon they would sail for France. Emotions were close to the surface and a sense of dedication to a cause was felt by far more of the men than would seem possible to today's less romantic generations. It would perhaps have been difficult to persuade any of the tough ex-Regulars to admit that they looked on the Colour as a favour given to their charge by a fair princess. Suffice it to say that they prized it and carried it into every battle which the Regiment fought in the First World War. To all members of the Regiment it is known affectionately as the 'Ric-a-dam-doo'.

On Friday, 28 August, the Regiment boarded the liner *Megantic* at Montreal, bound for England. It was seventeen days since the first call for recruits had been made. The target which Col Farquhar and Major Gault had set themselves had been achieved. They sailed next morning but at Quebec, a new authority intervened. The Admiralty had decided that no troops might cross the Atlantic except in convoy. The Patricias were to wait until the First Canadian Contingent was ready. They disembarked and camped at Levis.

A month of training ensued before they boarded ship again. On 18 October, after three weeks at sea, the Regiment arrived at Bustard Camp on Salisbury Plain. At an inspection by the King, Hamilton Gault formally handed over the Regiment to his service.

In mid-November, the Patricias moved to Winchester to join four British regular battalions returning from India to form the 80th Infantry Brigade. They were the 2nd Battalion, King's Shropshire Light Infantry, the 3rd and 4th Battalions, King's Royal Rifle Corps and the 4th Battalion, Rifle Brigade. Thus began the Regiment's association with the Green Jackets.

The 80th Brigade formed part of the 27th Division of the new V Corps which was being organized under the command of Gen Sir Herbert Plumer. When they crossed to Le Havre on 21 December, theirs was the ninth division to join the BEF. Not one of the Patricias could have imagined on that hot August day when they left Ottawa that it would be four long months before they arrived in France. Nor could they have foreseen the wet, the cold and the mud of southern England's most miserable autumn in living memory. Now at last they were in France which was where they wanted to be and they were in no mood to be depressed by what they found there. This was fortunate.

The transit camp at Le Havre was as uninviting as anything on

Salisbury Plain. After another night in the cold and wet, they were delighted to board a train for St Omer. That short journey took twenty-four hours, which were spent confined in typical French box cars. With forty men to a truck, it was not possible for all to sit down at the same time, and as one veteran noted, 'Some promising friendships were strained by this arrangement.' The guide who met the battalion at Arques lost his way and the men were not amused when at three o'clock in the morning after a long march, they found that they must retrace their steps for more than two miles. Billets for the next few days were in the village of Blaringhem and its surrounding farms. Bully beef was served for Christmas dinner.

The Hazebrouck defensive line was being constructed in the area and the Patricias spent the last week of the year digging trenches in the water-logged soil of Flanders. Sir John French inspected them on New Year's Day and on 5 January they marched towards Ypres. The Battalion waited for dusk to come in a sodden field near Dickebusch before moving forward to the front line to relieve the 53rd Regiment of the 32nd French Division.

The experience of the Patricias that night was in no way unique for a unit of the BEF. Much has been written of the miseries of trench warfare in the First World War, but at no time were conditions worse than they were in the Ypres salient during that first winter. The Battalion's position was dominated by those of the enemy which were on higher ground. There were no communication trenches leading to the rear and it was impossible to move either in or out of the trenches in daylight. These were mere ditches dug across a sea of mud, too wide to provide protection from shell fire and too shallow to be bullet proof. In places a man would be waist deep in water if he were to stand in the bottom of the trench. They could not be drained, hence they could not be deepened. The walls collapsed from lack of revetting. There were no sand bags with which to build a proper parapet. Unburied bodies lay in front and behind them and the area was infested with rats.

It is impossible to equip men to be comfortable under such

conditions. At that time there was a shortage of boots and many men had worn completely through the soles of theirs. The Army had not learned to cope with 'trench foot' and the casualties from exposure were as high among the Patricias as among soldiers who had come direct from India. On the first day in the line, 7 January, 1915, the Regiment lost its first two men killed in action. In the first six weeks of trench warfare, the Patricias suffered 70 battle casualties. At one point however, they were 400 under strength because of sickness.

In the circumstances, it was easy for troops to become over-impressed with the quality of the enemy. The German positions were better sited and their trenches drained into those of the Allies. Far more shells and bombs were falling on them than on the Germans. A constant toll of casualties was taken by the aggressive enemy snipers.

Few options were open to a commanding officer under these circumstances, but Col Farquhar made the most of them. As a start he organized a sniping section under the scout officer, Lieut W. G. Colquhoun and Cpl J. N. Christie. He gave them a free hand and told them to fight the Germans with their own weapons. From the outset they were successful, in one two-day period accounting for seventeen of the enemy.

Christie was the most durable of men. He came from the Yukon where he had been a bear hunter. In one encounter with a grizzly, his jaw and the left side of his head were nearly torn off and he had had to finish the bear with his knife. It took him five days to reach civilization and medical treatment. He was over 40 years old when he joined the Regiment, an advanced age for an infantry-man in the field.

Lt-Col H. W. Niven writes of him as follows: 'His long life alone in the mountains made him the most observant man I have ever known. He saw everything and said nothing. He could put his hand on the ground in no man's land and tell whether a man had walked there one hour ago, two hour's ago, three hours ago. It was uncanny, and he was never wrong. He would lie out in the open behind our trenches, day after day . . . and get his sight on some part of the enemy trench and wait for someone to put his head up. If he did not put it up today, he would be there tomorrow, and sure enough some German would come to that spot, and Christie would get him. This happened year after year. I have never known anyone outside an Indian who had the patience of Christie. He would concentrate hour after hour on one spot. No white man that I know of can concentrate for more than say, three hours on one spot. Christie could do it for two days. Everything told him a story – a bent blade of grass told him something.

'Christie wandered over no man's land all night long, and he came back one morning saying that he thought a German patrol went past our front about 2 am. He wanted four men to go out next night to scupper the lot. I rode into Headquarters and spoke to Gen Sir George Milne (afterwards CIGS – 'Uncle George' to the PPCLI) who said he would come along about midnight.

'About 2 am a hell of a row started away to our left front in no man's land. We could not fire and neither could the Germans as we both had patrols out. About 3.30 am Christie and his men came in and Uncle George questioned them.

'Christie and his men had lain out in the open ground each with four grenades and his rifle. The German patrol, one officer and sixteen men came across where Christie thought they would. First he shot the officer, each of his men threw two Mills bombs and finished them off with their rifles. Then Christie cut off their shoulder straps for identification and put them in a sand bag, and put all the officer's papers etc in. But Christie was in a state of consternation. He found that his patrol had pinched the German rifles and two of his men had left their own. Christie asked Sir George for permission to go out and get the rifles as he was responsible. The General's face was a study, but he gave permission and he awarded Christie an immediate DCM.'

Christie remained in charge of the snipers until the end of June, 1918, when he finally left the Battalion as a lieutenant.

On 27 February, Col Farquhar found another way to hit at the enemy. The Germans opposite them were digging a fire trench close to one of the Patricias' positions. It seemed likely that it was designed as a jumping off place for an attack upon their defences. Farquhar asked for permission to deliver a local attack against it. This 'reconnaissance in force' is of some historic importance as it was the first engagement fought by a Canadian regiment on the continent of Europe. It was also the first of those 'trench raids' which become the hall mark of the Canadian Corps during the next three years. As the regimental history notes 'all the essentials of subsequent raids were present: the sudden assault by a handful of troops on a small section of line; the division of the attacking force into small groups, each with a special task; the systematic destruction of a trench; the attempt to secure prisoners for identification; the withdrawal before the enemy could counter-attack after inflicting upon him all possible damage.' At 5.15 am the assault party dashed across the 15 to 20 yards of no man's land and, turning to the right, cleared the length of the trench. The supporting party moved along in its rear to prevent interference from the German communication trenches. The third group pulled down as much as they could of the laboriously constructed parapet. The whole affair was over in less than half an hour.

This brilliant little action was good for everyone's morale in the midst of that cold and discouraging winter. The Regiment received congratulations from no less than the Brigade, Divisional, Corps and Army Commanders and from the Commander-in-Chief himself. Farquhar was pleased with his men, as they were with him. More and more too, they liked what they saw of Major Hamilton Gault. Early on the night of the raid, he had crawled around to the rear of the German position and examined the ground between it and the enemy main trench system to fix the position of the communication trenches which connected them. Later he was wounded while crossing open ground in front of the Patricia position under heavy aimed fire, carrying a man who had been hit during the raid.

The enemy were less well pleased. All next day the Patricias' trenches were under heavy fire and the two days' operations brought them over 70 casualties. The Battalion remained in the area of St Eloi until the 23 March, garrisoning the line, providing working parties and taking part in a limited counter attack near the Mound. It suffered many casualties. On the night of 19/20 March the battalion was relieved. Later that night Col Farquhar was wounded as he was taking the commanding officer of the relieving unit around the position. He was carried back safely, but died in a forward dressing station. His funeral took place the following night in the Regimental cemetery outside Voormezeele. It was a black night and the neighbouring fields and roads were under constant fire. So dangerous was it that officers and men approached the cemetery in groups of two or three. Only 40 were allowed to attend. Canada owes a great debt to the British Army for producing officers like Francis Farquhar.

Talbot Papineau, brilliant descendant of the great French Canadian patriot wrote, 'As a Canadian I feel a debt of gratitude to him. An Imperial officer who could have commanded the highest position in the English army, he accepted the task of creating, as well as commanding a new and untried Canadian regiment. He knew well how to combine the discipline and dignity of the regular British Army with the easy independence and democracy of a volunteer Colonial regiment. At all times he exercised a tact and kindness which removed difficulties or overcame them. He, more than any other, has given us a reputation and a standard which we must strive to maintain.

'I was anxious to do well in order to please him. In the firing line his coolness and courage had a great effect on me. I hardly felt any nervousness if I were with him, and I had entire confidence in his judgement.'

On 23 March, the Regiment left the St Eloi area to move to the centre of the Ypres Salient. In less than three months the Patricias had suffered 238 battle casualties in addition to the losses from sickness. Only 10 of the 27 officers were left. Major Hamilton Gault was in hospital with his wounds, and Capt H. C. Buller, the Adjutant and senior officer in the field, was promoted to command.

The Patricias entered Ypres for the first time on 5 April, 1915. When, more than three years later, they finally left this densely populated area of Belgium, the towns were piles of rubble and the fields were quagmires of stinking mud. No trees remained and very little grass. But at this time, away from the immediate vicinity of the front line trenches, towns were little damaged and were still inhabited. Woods and copses dotted the landscape. A combination of warm sunshine and the bright green leaves of spring raised the spirits of the men. When they found that the trenches which they were to occupy along the southern edge of Polygon Wood were almost dry and had decent parapets, they were delighted. War could be almost enjoyable in conditions so much better than those at St Eloi.

For the first two weeks, the area was relatively quiet. The Patricias were in reserve, billeted in the infantry barracks at Ypres, when the intensive preliminary bombardment for the forthcoming German offensive began. The barracks soon became unsafe and all day on 20 April the Regiment watched the systematic destruction of the city from outside its walls. That evening they moved back to the Polygon Wood trenches at the point of the Ypres Salient. There they remained for 12 days under constant shellfire during which they suffered 80 casualties. In the meantime, the heavy German attacks on the north of the Salient (during which poison gas was used for the first time) had so bent the line that the 80th Brigade were ordered to withdraw so that they would not be outflanked. They were to establish a defensive position along Bellewaerde Ridge, the last small rise in the ground to the east of Ypres. All troops were back on the new position by 3 o'clock in the morning of 4 May and began to prepare defences.

The German follow-up was done in classical style. Scouts, vanguard, advanced guard, and flankers were seen coming over the opposite ridge. So impressive was the demonstration, that to quote the regimental history 'all the men stood upon the parapet to see the show, some of them waving their arms and cheering like mad, but the advance quickly lost interest as a spectacle, for the Germans pushed machine guns within 200 yards and bullets were soon raking the parapets.' The Patricias watched from behind cover as the main guard deployed in the open at the double, helpless to interefere since no artillery could be brought to bear.

Soon the Germans began an intensive bombardment of the Patricias' position, and by 10 o'clock that night when they were relieved they had suffered a further 122 casualties. Next day Col Buller was wounded by a shell splinter. Fortunately Major Hamilton Gault had returned two days before from hospital and was in command when the Patricias moved forward on the evening of 6 May to relieve the Shropshires on the Bellewaerde and Frezenberg Ridges.

The first German assault of the 2nd battle of Ypres had been launched on 22 April behind a cloud of chlorine gas. That which fell on the Patricias and their comrades of the British 27th and 28th Divisions, was preceded by the heaviest and most intensive artillery bombardment which the Germans could devise. Survivors said they saw nothing to equal it again in the First World War. It began at about 7 am. Shrapnel and enfilading machine gun fire were devastating to the garrisons of the inadequate trenches. Shells blew in whole bays at a time. The main assault was launched at 9 am and was beaten back mainly by rifle fire. All day the Germans kept up the pressure, mounting attack after attack, each preceded by accurate concentrations of artillery fire. Casualties were appalling. By noon ammunition was running short and a gallant company of the Rifle Brigade came forward through the artillery fire with boxes of ammunition and two machine guns. They were deployed on the left flank from whence the 83rd Brigade had completely disappeared. At about 3 pm when a platoon of the Shropshires brought forward more ammunition and were deployed in the trenches, 80% of the Patricias were casualties. They had no machine guns and little ammunition. Five officers were left and they were commanded by a wounded captain. There was a great gap on the left flank and the holes and ditches which the remnants of the battalion occupied were under fire from three sides. Shortly afterwards a final German assault was beaten back and about 5 pm the artillery fire ceased. The 3rd Battalion King's Royal Rifle Corps relieved what was left of the Regiment, four officers and 150 men.

During the second battle of Ypres, 22 April to 17 May, 700 all ranks were killed, wounded or missing in action, the longest casualty list in the 27th Division. It marked the end of the 'Originals' as the core of the Regiment. They had begun the battle under the command of their founder, Hamilton Gault. He was hit early in the day, but continued in command until after the second German assault when he was again wounded so badly that he was unable to move about the line. A captain succeeded him, then a lieutenant. Companies were commanded by corporals, platoons by privates. Cohesion remained, as one would expect in a battalion of old regulars.

Chapter 2

The University Men

FOR the ten days after 8 May there was no respite for the survivors. They were formed into a composite unit with the remains of the 4th King's Royal Rifle Corps and on 14 May were back in the line at Hooge Château. On 18 May reorganization began under Lt-Col R. T. Pelly who had returned from sick leave and been promoted to command. He was faced with a formidable problem.

No provision had been made by the Canadian Government for replacing the casualties of the PPCLI. The Regiment had been privately raised and must find its own reinforcements. A small number had come to England with the Regiment where they had remained when it came to France. Other small drafts had joined them there, but many of these had been absorbed by the unit to replace the casualties they had suffered earlier in the year. Toward the end of May, 1915, 450 men were supplied from Canadian battalions in England.

It was apparent soon after the Regiment first went into action that if they were to remain in existence, a constant flow of reinforcements would be needed. Friends in Canada solved the problem by recruiting through the universities. Six companies were formed from this source. The Students Union at McGill was their mobilization centre and as a result the 'University Companies Reinforcing PPCLI', as they were officially known, were often referred to as the 'McGill Companies'. In fact, every university in Canada contributed its fair share of professors, graduates and undergraduates. The first of these arrived at the end of July to join the battalion at Armentières. The second came on 1 September, and the men of three more were with it when it fought at Sanctuary Wood and on the the Somme in 1916.

By that time however, the Patricias were part of the Canadian

Corps and were provided with further drafts from the normal reinforcement system.

The supply of officers was not a concern. In 1915 it was not usual for men to be commissioned from the ranks in their own unit – usually they went to another. However, Col Farquhar had departed from this practice from the outset. The Regiment never lacked for officer material within its own ranks. From the autumn of 1916 to the end of the War, practically all its officers were found from this source. In all 335 men were commissioned from the ranks of the PPCLI in the field, two-thirds of them for other Canadian and British units.

The old soldiers of the PPCLI viewed the university men with wonder. At about the time when the first of them arrived, jam had become a more or less regular part of the rations issued to the troops. The enterprising 'old sweats' traded it for wine, but the new men actually ate it! Some were even known to have stated a preference for milk over beer. But the two groups got on well together, as the reinforcements showed how quick they were to learn the hard-won facts of war.

For the Patricias the summer of 1915 was the quietest they spent in France. For three months they were constantly in the line near Armentières but suffered only 15 casualties. From there, they moved to the Somme for six weeks, only two of which they spent in the line. This was the last time they were in contact with the enemy as part of the 80th Brigade.

It was no longer possible for the British Army to maintain brigades of five battalions, so one of the 80th's would have to go to another formation. The lot fell to the Patricias since the 27th Division had been ordered to Salonika where it would be difficult to reinforce a Canadian Regiment. The decision lay between joining another British brigade or joining the new 3rd Canadian Division which was to be formed in France. Remarkably the decision seems to have been left to the Regiment.

When the PPCLI was formed most of the men had been born in the British Isles, but now the majority were of Canadian birth. Worries concerning the supply of reinforcements might easily arise again. To Col Pelly, Major Gault and Col Buller the answer was clear. On 8 November, they left to join the Royal Canadian Regiment and the 42nd and 49th Battalions of the Canadian Expeditionary Force in forming the 7th Canadian Infantry Brigade. The new formation was not to come into existence officially until 22 December. In the meantime, the Patricias were brought up to strength and for two weeks, acted as demonstration battalion at the Third Army Officer's School.

The Officer's Mess was in the Château de Flixecourt where one evening, they gave a dinner for M. Saint, the owner. The Pipe Major came in to play for the officers and did his best to produce the Marseillaise. Nobody recognized it except M. Saint who rose and stood to attention. After a moment, the bewildered officers did likewise, convinced that French customs at Mess dinners were even more mysterious than their own.

On 7 December, Col Buller returned and Col Pelly was given command of the 8th Royal Irish Rifles. On 12 January, 1916, the Patricias were back in the line at the southern end of the Ypres Salient, less than two miles from where they had first seen action a year before. The next two months were relatively quiet, but in the middle of March the Regiment moved, as they had done almost a year before, through Ypres and entered the front line in Sanctuary Wood. They were only 700 yards from where the Originals died on Frezenberg Ridge and were at the eastern tip of the Ypres Salient. There followed two months of manning the trenches opposite a well-trained and aggressive enemy.

In May, 1915, if the Patricias had not stopped them, the Germans could have taken Ypres. The position which they held at the beginning of June, 1916, was of equal tactical importance. Looking back on the battle which they fought there and the events which preceded it, it is possible to draw many parallels with the experience of the year before. It was almost as if the university men were being tested to see if they could match the performance of the Originals.

There was, however, a curious difference in the German intentions for the two battles. The battle of Frezenberg, 1915, had been part of the second battle of Ypres when the whole weight of the German Army had been directed to the capture of the city. The battle of Sanctuary Wood was designed to restore the reputation of the commander of the 13th Wurtemberg Corps. He had recently been censured for failure and he needed a dramatic success. He was determined to capture Mount Sorrel and Observatory Ridge, which completely dominated the low-lying ground which lay between them and Ypres. The Patricia position in Sanctuary Wood blocked one of the approaches to these features, which were held by the 8th Canadian Infantry Brigade.

The enemy preliminary bombardment was again so heavy that the right forward company position was soon obliterated. All communications to the rear were cut and the battalion was isolated by a curtain of fire. Few of the right-hand company survived the bombardment and their position was over-run in the enemy's first assault, as were those of the two battalions on their right. The Germans started to advance along the communication trenches toward the vital support line. There followed a murderous battle for the successive blocks which the defending platoons threw in their path. Parties of the enemy had penetrated through the battalion on the right and were moving toward the rear of the Patricias. Thus the early afternoon found No 4 Company of the battalion deployed to protect the rear, with two of its platoons clearing trenches and woods of the enemy, and half of No 3 Company being slowly wiped out in the defence of the communication trenches. From its original position on the left of the front line, No 2 Company, completely isolated, its officers all killed or wounded, was pouring fire into the enemy's right rear and upon his reserves moving forward in support. Col Buller gathered together the remaining two platoons of No 3 Company, men from battalion headquarters and the few remnants of No 1 Company to fight their way to the front along the communication trenches and join up with the two hard-pressed platoons defending them. He was shot dead directing the advance. Almost immediately thereafter his men reached the defenders of the communication trenches and blocked the German assault.

The enemy's drive slackened and the remaining positions of the battalion were again subjected to a very heavy bombardment. Three times during the night, the Wurtembergers assaulted No 2 Company. It was evident that, as they were running out of ammunition and as there was no hope of relieving them, they would have to be withdrawn to the support line. Shortly before daybreak, with a new attack developing, the company withdrew over the open fields, bringing with it all its ammunition, stores, machine guns and wounded, crossed 500 yards of open country, passed through an enemy barrage and reached the support line without the loss of a man.

Early on 3 June, other battalions counter-attacked through the Patricia position but suffered terribly in the process. Some of the men were relieved that night, but most did not move to the rear until after darkness fell on 4 June. The battalion had over 400 casualties, 19 of the 23 officers engaged being hit. The Commanding Officer was killed and Major Gault lost a leg and was never able to serve in the front line again.

The university men had shown themselves to be the equals of the old Regulars, but had lost most of their numbers in proving it.

The Patricias were hard at work, reorganizing and training on 13 June, when the 1st Canadian Division recaptured all the ground which had been lost. Next day the commander of the 13th Wurtemberg Corps was relieved of his command.

For another three months the battalion remained in the Ypres Salient, returning frequently to the line at its eastern tip between Hooge, Sanctuary Wood and Mount Sorrel. At the request of the Regiment, Col Pelly returned to take command. One more complete university company joined the Patricias in the field, but the bulk of the reinforcements now were to come from the general Canadian reserve in England.

At the end of August, the battalion moved to a training area on the Franco-Belgian border near Kassel, to train for the attack. In its twenty months at the Front, the Regiment had yet to take part in an offensive. There was much to be learned and the men enjoyed it. Their morale was high and they were full of confidence when they set off for the Somme on 7 September.

Chapter 3
Volunteers and a Few Pressed Men

A FTER the battle of Sanctuary Wood, the Patricias found their replacements from the same sources as other battalions of the Canadian Corps. Until the spring of 1918, these were volunteers but thereafter came many who had been conscripted under the controversial Military Service Act. They came from all parts of Canada and from all walks of life. Most were native-born Canadians. In the words of Herbert Fairlie Wood, 'In the appalling intimacy of the stinking trenches, they became profane, sceptical and irreverent. Quite unused to war or to the discipline of peace-time soldiering, they endured the experience because they thought they had to, but nothing could make them like it.'

In the course of the War, more than 50 officers and 500 men appeared in the casualty lists more than once. Many were wounded as many as five or six times, returning to the Regiment when they had recovered. For much of the War most of the officers had served under Col Farquhar and proved to be a firm base on which to maintain the Patricias' fighting traditions.

In the summer of 1916, a surprising number of Originals were still in uniform, either in France or in England. 171 were with the Regiment and more than 300 were recovering from wounds or were with other units.

In the opinion of many in the CEF, the PPCLI were a 'lucky battalion', as if anyone caught up in the First World War could be considered so. In the main though, the Patricias did not consider that they had any real ground for complaint about the fortunes of war. They were glad, for example, that they had to spend less than a month on the Somme.

The Regiment's first attack took place on the opening day of the battle of Flers-Courcelette. The initial phase had gone surprisingly well and, far sooner than they expected, the Patricias were called

The P.P.C.L.I. Comedy Company as it appeared at a command performance in London. Standing, left to right: T. J. Lilly, Fred Fenwick, J. W. McLaren, William Filson, Norman Nicholson and Charles Hillman. Seated: Lieutenant C. Biddulph and C. Stephens.

11. *The PPCLI Comedy Company as it appeared at a Royal Command Performance in London in 1918.*

12. *Farewell Parade for the Colonel-in-Chief, Bramshott, Surrey, 1919.*

13. *The Battle of Britain, 1940. PPCLI anti-aircraft detachment in position in Surrey.*

14. *Col Colquhoun inspects the Regiment at Cove, preparatory to intended operations in Norway.*

forward from Corps reserve to capture part of an old German defensive line called Fabeck Graben. There was no time for preliminary reconnaissance. Orders were to advance up a sunken road which led toward the enemy position. About a thousand yards before it, they would find an old trench running off at right-angles to the left. By filing along it, and facing to the right, the assaulting companies would be in line with and parallel to the Fabeck Graben.

Shell-fire had completely obliterated any sign of the trench along which they were to deploy. The Patricias found themselves well beyond it at zero hour, and there was nothing to do but deploy to the left over the open fields in broad daylight, within 500 yards of the enemy's position. As if that were not enough, the attack involved two changes in direction and the only land mark remaining was the flaming village of Courcelette on their right. Incredibly they got away with it and seized their objectives.

Some three weeks later, as the Patricias were leaving the Somme, they passed General Gough, the Army Commander, on the road. He called the Commanding Officer to him and asked him 'to inform all ranks that their clean, smart and soldierly appearance did the battalion the greatest credit. He was delighted to see a battalion coming out of the line showing such proof of discipline and efficiency'.

Two weeks later, they were holding a line of trenches about 900 yards long, on the western edge of Vimy Ridge and to these they returned for twelve successive tours. It was from these same positions that they later assaulted the Ridge in the great Canadian Corps attack of April, 1917.

The enemy line was less than 75 yards away and was separated from them by a series of huge craters. The Regiment had gained a reputation for patrolling and trench raiding, and these were features of each of their tours in the line. During this period, Col Pelly left to command the 91st British Infantry Brigade which he led at Passchendaele and later in Italy. He was succeeded by Lt-Col Agar Adamson, one of the original officers, who had commanded the battalion as a captain for much of the day at Frezenberg. He had been wounded there and had returned in

September, 1915. Apart from that break, he served continuously with the battalion in the field from January, 1915 to 27 March, 1918.

When they were not in the line, the Patricias spent their time in the routine of working parties, training and rest. They played football and baseball when they could, and were amused by the 'PPCLI Comedy Company', their own highly successful vaudeville group. There were military competitions of various sorts, and the battalion took a remarkable pride in its transport, which was very successful in horse shows organized in the BEF. Lt-Col H. W. Niven wrote that 'hundreds of men of the battalion used to walk up to five miles to see the transport perform. Can you imagine men walking that far voluntarily to watch trucks?'

When the Regiment was formed, they were given superb horses by wealthy and patriotic friends. The transport section was manned by cowboys and other professional horsemen, in marked contrast to so many other units whose sections were formed from the men that company commanders felt they could most easily spare. Not once during the War did the transport of the Patricias fail to get through to the unit with rations and ammunition.

The Royal Canadian Regiment were also proud of their transport. In January, 1917, the British Director of Veterinary Services reported 'The PPCLI and RCR are without doubt exceptional in their proficiency in the care of their animals, harness, limbers and standings . . . I have yet to see transport to equal that of these battalions either in the Imperial or Canadian Armies.'

The assault of 9 April, 1917, on Vimy Ridge was the only time in the First World War that the Patricias went 'over the top' at zero hour of a great offensive, and it was a model of what a set-piece attack should be. There was careful reconnaissance, intensive training, and meticulous rehearsal. No longer were the infantry to advance steadily in long lines to the objective, come what may. New flexibility was allowed in their tactics, permitting them to take advantage of what cover the ground provided and to move forward using fire and movement.

At 5.30 am the pipers played them over the top. The battalion advanced into the craters in front of them and through the German front line which had been obliterated by the preparatory bombardment. As they penetrated deeper into the enemy positions, there was resistance but the new tactics were successful and they seized their second objective with less than 50 casualties.

The battalion suffered heavily, however, in the next two days from shelling and sniping. Before it was withdrawn it had lost 222 men. As the regimental historian has pointed out, it is a paradox that complete successes make less history, in the case of small units at least, than do failures.

For the next few months, the battalion stayed in the area of Vimy Ridge and in the line near Lens. At one point in this period, to their delight, Major Hamilton Gault, DSO, was given command of the Regiment in the field, despite his disability, while the Commanding Officer was on leave.

The Canadian Corps moved back to the Ypres Salient in October to take part in the battle of Passchendaele. Gen Currie little relished commiting his Corps in an attempt to resuscitate a campaign that was already played out. Their objective was the 165-foot high ridge which ran through the village of Passchendaele. The water courses and drainage system had been so disrupted by shell fire that nearly half the area in front of the village was covered with water or deep mud. The Patricias' objectives lay along the north side of the bog and included several groups of pill-boxes – reinforced concrete machine gun positions with walls five feet thick. General Currie's note, 'battlefield looks bad, no salvaging has been done and very few of the dead buried' was an understatement. The Patricias would have to cross 2,000 yards of it.

As they 'jumped off' through the sea of slime, the pipers were unable to play for the beginning of one of the most desperate days in the Regiment's history. Soon the casualties reached appalling proportions. The advance became a series of small section and platoon battles around the German strong-points and pill-boxes. Snipers on both sides accounted for many casualties. Most of the Regiment's losses came from this source, but it was largely the accuracy and enterprise of the Patricia riflemen beating down the fire of the pill-boxes and machine gun nests that enabled the battalion to advance.

Moments before his company was to begin their attack toward Meetcheele village, Major Talbot Papineau turned to the second-in-command Major H. W. Niven, DSO, MC, and remarked, 'You know, Hughie, this is suicide.' By the time they reached their intermediate objective, there were 40 men left commanded by the wounded Company Sergeant Major. Papineau was dead. There were fewer still and a corporal was in command as they closed on the pill-box on the ridge which barred their advance. The artillery had not touched it and there seemed no way to advance in the face of the machine guns which fired from every embrasure.

Three of the oldest Patricias appeared on the scene, all of them veterans of Frezenberg – Lt J. M. Christie, DCM, Sgt G. H. Mullin, MM, of the Regimental Snipers and Lt Hugh MacKenzie, DCM, of the Brigade Machine Guns. There was little time to take the pill-box. At the rate casualties were occurring, there would soon be no one left to assault it. Christie ran and crawled forward on the left to a position where he could bring his deadly fire to bear on the pill-box and the sniper posts around it. MacKenzie turned over the command of his machine guns to an NCO and took charge of the men of his old Regiment. After a quick reconnaissance, he dashed from shell hole to shell hole to organize the assault. As his small party rushed up the slope, machine guns in the pill-box concentrated their fire upon them and MacKenzie was killed. Meanwhile, Sgt Mullin crawled up the slope and took the pill-box single-handed. He rushed a sniper's post in front and destroyed the garrison with bombs. Then, crawling onto the top of the pill-box, he shot the two machine gunners with his revolver. Mullin then rushed to another entrance and compelled the garrison of ten to surrender. His clothes had been riddled by bullets, but miraculously he was not wounded. Lt MacKenzie and Sgt Mullin won the Regiment's first Victoria Crosses.

Gradually the battalion clawed forward and was able to consolidate a position on the ridge where they remained almost 36 hours under heavy fire and beat off three enemy counter-attacks.

On 6 November, the 1st and 2nd Canadian Divisions took Passchendaele itself and a week later the Patricias were back in the line north of the village. There they suffered heavy shelling and frequent strafing attacks by German aircraft on their uncompleted trenches. On the 20th, they left the Ypres Salient for the last time, leaving behind 750 of their dead.

The Regiment was not to see another major battle until the summer of 1918. The intervening months were spent in training and periods of defensive trench warfare. In the new year, Lt-Col Agar Adamson, DSO, left after 18 months in command and was succeeded by Major C. J. T. Stewart, DSO, the last remaining original officer with the battalion. On the 22 February, the King appointed Her Royal Highness, the Princess Patricia of Connaught to be Colonel-in-Chief of the Regiment.

The regimental history describes the December and January tours in the trenches as catch-as-catch-can street fighting in the streets and railway sidings of Lens and wryly remarks that 'as usual on Christmas Day, there was no Christmas dinner (indeed the Regiment never during the war had a chance to observe the festival properly on the right day)'. In March and April they were in the line in and near Avion.

The great Ludendorff 'drive' began on 21 March and it was not long before reports of the German successes reached the Regiment. The Patricias' tour in the trenches was extended. L/Cpl J. W. McLaren of the PPCLI Comedy Company has written about one of the more unusual events that occurred at that time.

'All the available troops were called back to front line duty, and we cleaned our rifles and polished our brass, ready to go back to our companies. After some days, a messenger finally came, and I was ordered to report to the Colonel. Imagine my surprise when I was handed an order, not for the trenches, but to take the Concert Party to London for a Command performance. I'll never understand the Army. Here we were in the middle of a decisive battle when every man was needed, and we were ordered to London. Back with the company, the boys wouldn't believe it until the trucks arrived to take our props to storage, the tailor came to fit our new outfits, and sundry brass hats drilled us on the correct behaviour when confronted with Royalty.

'On arrival in London, we were put up at the Regent Palace Hotel where everything was on the house except reanimating beverages – a far cry from the Somme and no rations. Ah, c'est la guerre! The great day finally arrived when we appeared at the Apollo Theatre before Royalty. We were enthusiastically received. The last of our five acts was a scene in Hell. Old Nick was seated on his throne, surrounded by his imps, and there came hurtling down a chute in turn such repulsive army characters as the sergeant-major, the paymaster, the sanitary man and the conscientious objector, each one of whom on arrival being sentenced to various fiery punishments. The last to arrive was Kaiser Bill himself, and when his satanic majesty was confronted by the War Lord, he immediately cringed and warped into snivelling submission and abdicated his throne in favour of the Kaiser, declaring he was an amateur compared to him. That was the end of the show, but when the cue line was given, the curtain stayed up. Kaiser Bill, on the throne, ventriloquised the message to the wings to drop the curtain. Nothing happened. Again the Kaiser, through clenched teeth entreated: Please, give us the curtain. Again nothing, so, stepping off the throne, he goose-stepped to the wings, and in a clarion voice that echoed through the theatre shouted: "Come on, Doc, drop the bloody curtain." The audience, including the Royal party, roared their approval. No finer denouement of a play could possibly be written.

'We had been told to get into our uniforms as quickly as possible after the show, to receive Royalty, but either the curtain calls took too long, or the royal party was too impatient, for they arrived in our dressing room while we were still in our bulbous army issue underwear. But the Royal party took the situation in its stride and carried on the usual chit-chat with nonchalance. What might easily have become embarrassing confusion turned into a loud buffo, when King George V, in parting, said to his Mary: "Come on, Doc, let's drop the bloody curtain and go." '

From January to July, 1918, the Regiment suffered only sixty casualties. The Canadian Corps and other British formations had been deliberately kept out of battle during this time so that they would be at the peak of their efficiency for the great offensives planned for the summer. These were to begin on 8 August with what the Commander-in-Chief loftily described as the 'disengagement of Amiens'.

The success of the initial attacks exceeded the wildest hopes. On the first day, Canadian formations were through the enemy defences and into the open country beyond. The Patricias, following up the advance of their brigade, rounded up prisoners including the commander of a German artillery brigade and his staff. The trenches seemed to have been left behind forever. But reserve formations, passing through, found their way blocked by fresh German divisions holding a three mile belt of trenches and wire which they had abandoned in 1917.

The story of the Regiment's attack on the village of Parvillers reads like so many other accounts of trench warfare. Bomb, bayonet and Lewis gun were the chief weapons used. At one point No 3 Company was completely isolated, far in advance of the troops on its flanks. A German battalion counter-attacked and when the company was almost surrounded, it was ordered to fight its way back. Sgt Robert Spall covered the withdrawal of his platoon by standing in the open and cutting down the advancing enemy with a Lewis gun. He moved back to join his men, and again when they were in danger of being cut off, he picked up another Lewis, jumped on to the parapet of a trench and held up the enemy with his fire until he was killed. He was awarded the Regiment's third Victoria Cross.

Eventually the German position was broken. The Regiment was withdrawn with the rest of the Corps, brought up to full strength and moved north to Arras. For the Patricias there followed the three day attacking battle for Jig Saw Wood. Slowly they advanced through another old German defensive position by the River Scarpe and suffered 60% casualties among the officers and 30% among the men before it was over.

The Canadian Corps' operations now followed the axis Arras to

Cambrai to Mons. The Patricias last major battle of the War was to be at Tilloy on the outskirts of Cambrai. And at last their luck was out.

On the afternoon of 26 September, the battalion was to move forward by rail to a concentration area for the attack. There they were to rest before beginning operations next day. But there was a derailment, a delay in obtaining buses, blocked roads and confusion and it was not until 7 am on the 27th that they were at their destination. With the rest of the 7th Brigade, they moved forward by easy stages during the day, prepared to pass through the leading Canadian divisions. They had had no rest when at 6 am on the 28th they moved off in close support of the attacking Royal Canadian Regiment. The plan was that when the leading battalions of the brigade reached the line of a light railway, the Patricias were to pass through and seize the village of Tilloy some 2000 yards beyond. Unfortunately the leading units were not successful and it was necessary to commit two companies of the Patricias to drive the enemy from their own start line. At 9.30 am Lt-Col Stewart, the Commanding Officer, was killed by a German shell and the command fell to Capt J. N. Edgar, who was commanding the right forward company.

Because of the stiffening resistance, the battalion's objective was altered by Brigade Headquarters to the line of another railway which crossed their front some 2000 yards away. The artillery had had difficulty in preparing the supporting barrage and when the attack began, their batteries were being heavily and accurately bombed by enemy aircraft. The supporting fire was inadequate.

Despite this the assault went well until, just short of their objective, they ran into that obstacle which had been the death of so many other good battalions in the First World War – two complete belts of uncut wire concealed from view by overgrown vegetation. Machine gun fire swept its length from covered enfilading positions and German guns covered the gaps. Desperate attempts to find a way through failed. There was nothing for it but to pull back the companies from their exposed position. It was a costly failure leaving Tilloy firmly in enemy hands.

There was little progress the next day. A new assault by the Patricias was planned for the 30th. The limits of the wire obstacle had been fixed and the battalion was able to outflank it, but by now the men were very tired. The objective was farther away than any allotted to a battalion at the outset of the battle and their rifle strength was little more than a company, but their blood was up. They took Tilloy. The unit which was to have seized the high ground dominating the village failed, leaving the Patricias exposed to German artillery firing over open sights, and to the concentrated fire of the machine gun posts on their flanks. Three tanks which were to accompany them in the attack were knocked out. For the next 12 hours, they held Tilloy. Completely unsupported and with both flanks in the air, they fought to clear the buildings on the outskirts. It was a battle to the finish with German troops determined to hold the dwindling number of roads to their units fighting in Cambrai. When at last the battalion was relieved, they left the line 140 strong, having suffered about the same number of casualties as they had at Passchendaele.

The Regiment was desperately crippled and the next month was devoted to training and bringing it back to something near the strength of a fighting battalion. Major A. G. Pearson, DCM, who had joined the Regiment in the field on 1 March, 1915, as a private, was given command with the acting rank of Lieutenant-Colonel.

For the last two weeks of October and the first few days of November, the 7th Brigade was in reserve. As the Canadian Corps moved toward the Belgian border on 7 November the Patricias at last found themselves in the van, about 12 miles west of Mons on the road from Valenciennes. It was a new experience for them as they advanced on a front of two miles – a force of all arms including a section of field guns and with a squadron of the 5th Lancers within call. They found the new role much to their liking.

During the next two days there were sharp little actions against enemy rearguards and they cleared several villages of the enemy. Everywhere they were greeted with delirious excitement by the French and Belgian civilians.

Soon they closed on Mons where in the outskirts, all but one company were to be relieved on the night of 9/10 November. The Germans seemed determined to hold the town. There was some fierce fighting and one company alone beat off five counter attacks. It was not until 10 am on the 10th that the relief was completed. During the day, No 4 Company PPCLI worked forward to within sight of the railway station and that night, with the 42nd Battalion and a company of the Royal Canadian Regiment, broke across the canal bridges into the city proper. It was cleared by 6 am. Shortly after daybreak, the 42nd Battalion was played through the city by their pipers, to the joy of the population.

At about 9 am a message was received at Battalion Headquarters announcing that an armistice would be effective at 11 am. Later that morning, the Patricias and the rest of the 7th Brigade paraded in the city. With them was a detachment of the 5th Lancers, who had been at Mons in August, 1914.

It seemed a pity to some that none of the infantry of the first hundred thousand, the Old Contemptibles, were present, but the end had come too quickly for such a gesture to history. The Patricias, through their 'Originals', were linked with almost every unit of the old British Regular Army. Thus, in a sense, all were represented that day on the city square of Mons.

Word of the armistice brought no wild scenes of joy in the Regiment. Rather it was received in silence, almost in disbelief. It seemed that men who had seen so much could not, on 11 November, bring themselves to rejoice in victory.

Putting the whole vast machinery of war into reverse is a slow process. The Regiment remained in Mons for a month, taking part in the ceremonials which marked the end of the war. For a week they provided the Royal Guard for King George V at his headquarters at Valenciennes. For another two months they remained in Belgium, and their last parade on the continent was held on 28 January, 1919, when the Camp Colour, which had been presented by Princess Patricia in 1914 was consecrated as the Regimental Colour. They sailed from Le Havre for England on 7 February, 50 months after they had landed. Their term of service exceeded that of any unit from overseas on the Western Front.

On 21 February there was a farewell parade for the Princess when she presented a Laurel Wreath in silver gilt to be borne on the Regimental Colour. On the 27th they mounted a Guard of Honour at her wedding in Westminster Abbey to Commander Alexander Ramsay, DSO, RN. King George had intended to inspect the Guard after the wedding, but in their enthusiasm at this first happy royal occasion after the War, the crowd surged forward through the police lines and literally carried the men off their feet. The Colonel-in-Chief later remarked 'it was indeed the only occasion in history on which the Regiment lost its ground.'

On 8 March, they sailed from Liverpool and on the 17th arrived in Halifax. Invitations to parade down Fifth Avenue in New York City and for a similar parade in Montreal were refused, and they proceeded direct to Ottawa for demobilization. There were addresses of welcome, a parade through the streets, an inspection by the Governor-General, then a final dismissal in Lansdowne Park, where the Regiment had been born on 11 August, 1914. Hamilton Gault said his farewell. He had been in command since Mons. Few of the Patricias that day knew what lay ahead for themselves, let alone for the Regiment, but years later, one of them wrote, 'we knew that we had lost something irreplaceable when on the tan bark of the Ottawa Horse Show Building, he dispersed us into civvy street'.

Chapter 4
The Permanent Force

A<small>T</small> the end of the First World War, there were few Canadians who would agree that the country needed a permanent military establishment, and fewer still who were prepared to become part of it. The patriotic fervour and sense of dedication which drew men to the war in its first few months was replaced, as it wore on, by the more sustaining impulse of a sense of duty. With the Armistice, emotions arose which had been suppressed or not realized throughout the War. There was a revulsion towards it and to all things military. Few families in Canada had been untouched by the casualty list. The fact that the United States of America had lost fewer men killed than had Canada did not go unnoticed. Canadians took pride in their sacrifice, yet many thought that they should not be quite so quick to jump next time.

But would there be a next time? Surely not! The opposition to government spending on defence was loud and widespread. In 1914, Canada had had a small regular force of 3,110 to train the part-time soldiers of the reserves. In 1920 even this figure seemed extravagant to many.

The Permanent Active Militia to give it its official title (or Permanent Force, as it was commonly called) consisted of two cavalry regiments, three infantry battalions and units of other arms and services. If it had been at full strength, Canada would have had more than 10,000 regulars. Strictures of economy and lack of interest on the part of the Government and people kept the numbers to around one-third of this. In the 1920's the average expenditure on the Permanent Force amounted to about $900.00 per man per year. This amount covered his equipment, rations and quarters as well as his training, his pay and provision for his pension. It left little scope for soldiering.

As early as 1916, thought was being given to the preservation of the PPCLI as a regiment after the War, probably as a battalion of the Permanent Force. The Regiment's superb fighting record was only one of the reasons it was finally selected for this role. The standard of so many war-time battalions had been so high that it would have been impossible to say which had been the best in the CEF. The record showed that 229 officers, and 4,857 other ranks had served in the PPCLI; the regiment suffered 228 and 3,848 casualties respectively, but many of these had been wounded more than once. Patricias had won three Victoria Crosses and 466 other decorations. But bloodshed and valour had been too common in the War to serve as a measure of comparison of the potential value of units to the Permanent Force.

The reason for the selection of the Patricias is not officially recorded, but the process is not difficult to imagine. Three infantry battalions were needed for the Permanent Force – one, the Royal Canadian Regiment, already existed. One should be French speaking – the choice naturally fell on the Royal 22e Regiment. All other battalions of the CEF with the exception of the Patricias were linked with a province or a district. Recruits from the Patricias had come from all parts of Canada and from every Canadian university. The circumstances of raising the Regiment, its name and its having been first to take the field, had caught the public imagination in all parts of Canada. Not only would it be a good selection, it would raise few political or emotional objections.

Hamilton Gault agreed to remain in the Service during the formative period of the peacetime battalion. He was joined by many old officers, NCOs and men. Until January, 1920, the PPCLI were stationed in Toronto and at nearby Long Branch Camp. That month they moved to Tecumseh Barracks in London, Ontario. Later in the year, the battalion moved to the West, to its permanent peacetime barracks. Headquarters, A and D Companies were quartered in Fort Osborne on the outskirts of Winnipeg and B Company in Esquimalt, near Victoria, British Columbia. Its fourth company was not raised until 1939.

Between the wars, the strength of the Regiment was never more than one-third of its war establishment and even this figure could not be maintained. From year to year it varied with the fluctuations in the restricted military budget of the country. To quote Col Niven again, 'In 1933, we received a wire from National Defence Headquarters telling me to discharge twenty men as they did not have enough money to pay them. As I had recruited these men, I felt that I had to get them jobs. I got Eatons and Hudson's Bay Company, Winnipeg, to take them on.

'In Esquimalt, I applied for $20.00 to buy paint to do the barrack rooms. It was refused by N.D.H.Q. I had to go to the Navy and beg the paint.'

Pay cuts, lack of equipment, restrictions on training, no money for maintenance, and no promotion typified life in the Permanent Force between the wars. Major-Gen C. B. Ware told how he first grasped the realities of peacetime soldiering when he joined the Regiment in 1935. Before graduating from the Royal Military College, he had read the first volume of the Regiment's history. He had been struck by the account of the vicious battle of Tilloy and of the distinguished part played in it by Capt J. N. Edgar, officer commanding A Company. When Lt Ware arrived at Winnipeg he was instructed by the Adjutant to report to A Company. There he was welcomed, 14 years after Tilloy, by the officer still commanding, Capt J. N. Edgar, MC.

But the experience of other veteran Patricia officers showed that Canada was not alone in restrictions on military advancement. Lt-Col R. T. Pelly left the Regiment in November, 1916, after commanding it with great distinction. Subsequently he was promoted to Brigadier-General and commanded a British infantry brigade on the Western and Italian fronts. He was awarded two DSOs, a CB, a CMG, an Italian *Croce di Guerra* and was mentioned in despatches seven times. He returned to the British Army after the war and found himself a junior captain in his regiment. By a quirk of the service, his new commanding officer had just been promoted to the rank of lieutenant-colonel for the first time, after a relatively undistinguished war-time career. Eventually Pelly resigned.

In the First World War, the mechanization of armies had begun. Motor transport was used extensively and tanks and other armoured vehicles had proved their value. The Canadian Motor Machine Gun Brigade had been a highly successful innovation. Progressive officers realized the potential of these developments, yet so little money was there, that the infantry and cavalry of the Permanent Force had no motorized vehicles at all. Horses provided the motive power of the army. Training exercises frequently became stereotyped affairs of horsed cavalry against marching infantry and usually ended with the cavalry putting in a charge for the edification of elderly generals and the enhancement of their own esprit. The veterans of the PPCLI, watching this sort of fantasy through the sights of their silent machine guns, found it ludicrous.

In the summer of 1923, the Patricias' irreverence for stylized military stupidity could be contained no longer and they decided to stop the nonsense. The final day of manoeuvres at Camp Hughes was drawing to a close. A cavalry brigade of the Non-Permanent Active Militia moved through the scrub bush and deployed into line in front of a wood facing the Patricias' position. A trumpet sounded and the Saturday night soldiers advanced in an admirable line, shoulder to shoulder, towards the infantry. Walk, trot, charge – their discipline was matched only by that of the foot, who as the cavalry drew near, rose from the ground as one man and pulled from their tunics sheets of newspaper which they waved in the eyes of the astonished horses. As one officer commented 'It was the greatest victory of infantry over cavalry since the Russians charged the 93rd at Balaclava.'

Unfortunately the G.O.C. was a cavalryman and it was some time before the Patricias heard the last of that incident.

Much as the Regiment would have wished for more modern transport, they enjoyed the army's horses. In Winnipeg with them was a squadron of Lord Strathcona's Horse and a battery of the Royal Canadian Horse Artillery. There were ample opportunities for mounted sports and the Regiment had several fine riders. It was significant that in this horsey garrison, it was the Patricias who for a time owned their own pack of draghounds.

With so little money for training, men of the Permanent Force spent more time at sports than is usual in the Army today and the Regiment produced several fine athletes. Rifle shooting, too, was inexpensive and popular. The Patricias were frequently represented at Bisley and collected an impressive cabinet of trophies.

The main occupation of soldiers of the Permanent Force was the training of the Non-Permanent Active Militia. (Canadian governments are partial to cumbersome euphemisms to describe their military forces. Soldiers spoke of the 'P.F.' and the 'Militia'.) Each Officer and NCO of the rank of corporal and above in the Patricias was trained as an instructor. For several months each year, they taught at officers' courses at the universities as well as holding schools for militiamen both at the Regiment's barracks and at other centres in Western Canada.

It was possible for the Regiment to maintain a high standard in the instruction given to the Militia for it was pitched at a junior level. But increasingly it became difficult to keep up the standard of higher tactical and operational training. Fortunately, some officers and NCOs were able to attend courses at Regular Army schools in Britain. But restricted strengths, and lack of equipment prevented the kind of experimentation and development of military thought which is so important to an army in peace.

On five occasions troops of the Regiment were called out to aid the civil power. Twice it was to contain riotous crowds of unemployed in Winnipeg, another time, to quell trouble in a penitentiary. On the fourth occasion, they helped to restore order in Sidney, Nova Scotia, after a strike of coal miners. The fifth time, in 1932, they were sent from Victoria to Vancouver to support the civil authorities but arrived to find that they were not needed.

Throughout the years there had been much ceremonial. Guards of Honour had been mounted at openings of Legislatures and for visiting Governors-General and the President of the United States. The Band was excellent and made tours of the United States and of Britain where they played at the Wembley Exhibition. The community liked what it saw of the Patricias, but for years the unmilitary Canadian did not want to become involved.

After the Armistice Day parade in Winnipeg in 1938, all the local papers commented on the Regiment's turn-out. This new interest marked the changing mood of the times. Col G. R. Stevens, OBE, author of Volume III of the regimental history noted that 'soldiers had begun to matter once more'.

Chapter 5
Volunteers Again

THE approach of war in 1939 was watched by the Canadian people in a very different frame of mind from that of 1914. This time the country knew what war meant. They were appalled at the march of events in Europe and angered by the recklessness of dictators in putting civilization at risk. On 25 August, when men of the Canadian Militia turned out to guard public buildings and other vital points, there was little swelling of pride or martial ardour among the people. When mobilization was ordered on 1 September, lines of volunteers appeared at recruiting stations but signs of wild enthusiasm were lacking. The men were serious.

The raising of two divisions in 1939 strained the country's military resources to the utmost. There were practically no reserves of equipment, even of rifles and uniforms. Infantry battalions in the Militia averaged 200 to 300 men and for the most part these were far from being trained for war. They had now to be brought up to full war establishment.

In 1938 the Patricias had 352 men on strength. When mobilization was ordered, one of the first tasks of the Regiment was to provide trained instructors for the expanding battalions of the Militia. It so depleted their ranks that their own mobilization suffered. Not until the end of October were they fully up to strength and it was 15 November when B and D Companies arrived from Esquimalt, that the battalion finally came together.

Many former officers and men returned to the Regiment. Lt-Col Hamilton Gault, who was in England, offered his services to the Canadian Government and was given command of an overseas reinforcement depot. Lt-Col Tenbroeke, a former CO, took command of the newly-formed Regimental Depot and the battalion itself had for its commander, the original intelligence officer of the

Regiment, Lt-Col W. G. Colquhoun, MC.

Until October, 1939, the Patricias' service uniform had been that of the First World War. In that month, battle dress was issued for the first time. They now marched three abreast instead of in fours, but they were to see few other changes from World War I practice in weapons and techniques until they went overseas.

In November it was announced that the Patricias, with the Edmonton Regiment and the Seaforth Highlanders of Canada from Vancouver, would form the 2nd Canadian Infantry Brigade, commanded by a distinguished former Patricia, Brig G. R. Pearkes, VC, DSO, MC. It, in turn, would be part of Major-Gen A. G. L. McNaughton's 1st Canadian Division.

On 5 December, the Regiment's advance party departed for Britain and on the 17th the battalion left Winnipeg. Four days later they sailed from Halifax on *HMT Orana*. Christmas was celebrated pleasantly enough at sea and on the 30th the convoy entered the Clyde. The Patricias disembarked at Greenock and by late afternoon were moving south on troop trains for Aldershot. On the last day of the year they arrived at Morval Barracks, Cove. It was bitterly cold, the pipes were frozen and there were only small paraffin heaters to dispel the chill. But the British people welcomed the Canadian troops warmly. Invitations poured in and it was not long before most Patricias had friends among them.

The battalion thawed the pipes in Morval Barracks, then got down to work. It was a busy period. At last the long-awaited new equipment began to arrive and the battalion learned to use it. Emphasis was placed on weapon training and tactics. Boosey and Hawkes, the London music supply house, loaned instruments to the Regiment so the stretcher bearers might become a band once again. The King inspected the Patricias with other units of the 1st Canadian Division on 24 January. Then on 10 February, Lady Patricia Ramsay, the Colonel-in-Chief, reviewed her Regiment for the first time in 21 years. These were the only ceremonial occasions, for the battalion's programme began to react to the realities of war.

So far, scarcely a shot had been fired by the British and French armies facing the Germans along their frontier. In March, however, the feeling grew that fighting must soon begin. The Regiment had learned that it was unlikely that the Canadians would go to France for some months. Yet the sense that something was about to happen spurred their efforts.

1940 was a spring of disasters for the Allies. They began on 9 April with the German attack on Norway and Denmark. Within 24 hours the enemy had over-run the latter and were firmly established in every major port in Norway. On the 12th, British troops sailed for Narvik. Four days later the 1st Canadian Division were asked to help in a direct assault on the port of Trondheim. The PPCLI and the Edmonton Regiment were selected for the operation. The Patricias were delighted to be picked for the first Allied land offensive of the war.

On 18 April the Battalion moved to Scotland, where they were issued with northern gear. The first rum issue of the war served to convince doubters that this was the real thing. By 21 April planners at the Admiralty and the War Office realized that the operation was impracticable and the Patricias were ordered to stand down. For three more days it seemed possible that they might be sent to Narvik instead. Then gloom descended upon the battalion. On the 24th, the order was received to turn in the special stores and equipment of the expedition and return to barracks.

Training was interrupted to hold a regimental Field Day on the 25th anniversary of the Battle of Frezenberg. The polo grounds at Fleet had been borrowed for the purpose and the Colonel-in-Chief presented the prizes. Next day a number of officers departed on leave but were recalled within 24 hours. The invasion of the Low Countries had begun. There was likely to be little time left for the battalion to learn its last tactical lessons before facing the enemy in the field.

The third week of May found the Patricias taking part in brigade training on Salisbury Plain. When they returned to Aldershot on the 26th they found the situation much changed. Two days earlier the 1st Brigade had begun to move to France, but the situation there had deteriorated so quickly that they were halted. Instead, General McNaughton had been asked to organize a self-contained

mobile force for the defence of the United Kingdom. Fresh equipment and vehicles were issued and on the 29th, the Patricias moved
to the small town of Kettering in Northamptonshire. For more than
a week they remained in that area, while in the Channel the
evacuation of Dunkirk was going on. As the great movement of men
and little ships continued, plans were made for opening a new front
in Brittany, using all available British and Commonwealth troops.
When the Patricias returned to Cove, they found that the first
detachments of the division were already on the move to France.
Hurried preparations were made to follow. The battalion's transport
embarked at Falmouth but before they could sail, it had become
apparent that the Brittany operation was a forlorn hope. The
battalion's movement order was cancelled.

Amazingly most of the British Expeditionary Force from the
Continent had been saved, though their equipment had been lost.
For a time the 1st Canadian Division was the only fighting
formation in the British Isles which was equipped and ready to do
battle. Once more it was given the role of a mobile force to repel
invasion and was stationed in the Oxford area.

On 23 June the Patricias bivouacked at Wotton Park, ten miles
north-east of Oxford and prepared for the fighting which all felt
must follow. General McNaughton had defined the role of the
Canadians as a central reserve operating on a 360 degree front.
In a surprisingly short time British divisions were reformed and
equipped and it became possible to have a mobile reserve both in
the north and the south. On 2 July the Patricias moved to the
Kentish Downs on the southern outskirts of London.

Earlier in the year a number of men from the Regiment had
gone to sea to man anti-aircraft machine guns on merchant shipping
in the English Channel, North Sea and North Atlantic. They had
had their share of adventures and one team of two Patricias rowed
an open boat from near Iceland to the Hebrides after their ship
had been sunk by gunfire from a German submarine. These crews
were the first Patricias to be in action against the enemy. They
returned to the battalion early in July.

Toward the end of the month the battalion moved to the area

of Godstone where they were to remain for more than a year. Their time was divided between training and operational tasks. Defences were constructed to meet the threat of invasion and the unit practised cooperation with artillery and tanks. Sometimes an unexpected note of realism was introduced into the exercises. More than once the Patricias' anti-aircraft machine guns engaged enemy raiders while the battalion was training.

At Godstone and Lingfield their billets lay on one of the flyways of German aircraft to London and there were frequent bombings as the Battle of Britain went on overhead. The battalion's first prisoner was a German pilot, brought down by the RAF. For four months air raids occurred almost daily. There was considerable damage to the battalion's quarters and equipment and on one occasion the unit's slit-trenches were machine-gunned by raiding aircraft. Men of the battalion fought fires and repaired bomb damage with their civilian neighbours. As the bombing increased, the spirits of the British grew. The Patricias were glad to be among them and helped where they could.

On 9 September, Col Colquhoun was promoted to command a brigade. He was the last original officer serving with the Regiment and it was a sad occasion when he left. Major J. N. Edgar, MC, was promoted to replace him, almost 22 years since the first time he had been in command of the battalion, at the Battle of Tilloy in September, 1918.

In November the battalion moved to Brighton to man the coastal defences for three weeks. Battalion headquarters was located at Roedean, the famous girls' school. It is recorded that they took the best of care of the appointments of the school, but that one fixture may have been over-worked. Some of the rooms had push-buttons with the notice, 'For a mistress, ring the bell'.

In Godstone on Christmas Day, they learned that the 2nd Canadian Division was now complete in England and that the 1st Canadian Corps had been formed. 1941 was another year of training. Almost every operation of war was practised. Toward the end of July, however, the unit became convinced that a forthcoming exercise called 'Heather' would be more than just another training scheme. The preparations seemed too realistic. On 6 August, they moved to Glasgow by rail and boarded *HMT Empress of Canada*. When the ship sailed later in the day the unit had not been briefed. On the 9th they landed and marched to camp at Inverary for mountain climbing and beach exercises. Four days later they re-embarked, returned to Glasgow, and boarded trains for Surrey. Exercise Heather was over.

Both the Patricias and the Edmonton Regiment, the two units disappointed at the time of the Trondheim expedition, had taken part in the exercise. When they learned that 'Heather' was to have been a raid on Spitzbergen, which was subsequently carried out by a much smaller expedition, the battalion was less than philosophical.

In 1941 the Patricias had four commanding officers. Lt-Col R. F. L. Keller, who succeeded Col Edgar on 18 June, and Lt-Col C. Vokes commanded for periods of only six weeks each. Both later rose to the rank of major-general and commanded divisions in action. Lt-Col R. A. Lindsay, who succeeded Col Keller, remained for two years.

In the latter part of August the Regiment moved to billets at Oxted and Limpsfield, a few miles east of Godstone. They remained there until the Regiment left Surrey for the last time to move to the south coast, east of Brighton.

By 1942, exercises were frequent and training was tougher and more realistic, with much use of live ammunition. The battalion became harder and fitter than ever. Officers were sent to North Africa for battle experience with the Buffs and the Coldstream Guards. In exercises like 'Tiger', the endurance of the men was tried to the utmost. They served only to sharpen their impatience to be in action. As one old soldier put it, 'War couldn't be that bad'.

A price had to be paid for the new realism however. Four men were killed in minefield accidents and three more when a shell dropped short in training. One soldier was wounded in the explosion of a mortar bomb. Early in August the Patricias again found themselves under attack by the Luftwaffe. In a series of noisy raids some of their billets were damaged and a Focke-Wulfe 190 was brought down by machine-gun fire.

On 19 August the battalion learned that the Dieppe Raid was in progress and felt some chagrin that they had been left out. Inevitably the feeling was somewhat tempered as they saw the first convoys of wounded return and talked to their friends in the 2nd Division. In January, 1943, the battalion was twice bombed and strafed on training by Focke-Wulfe aircraft. On the second occasion D Company brought one down by light-machine-gun fire within fifty yards of Beachy Head.

February found the battalion back in Inverary doing more amphibious training. They were told that 1943 was to be their year. Cynics doubted it. Shortly afterwards they returned to the outskirts of Eastbourne.

But there was not much longer to wait. On 17 March the Colonel-in-Chief visited the Regiment on her birthday. More exercises followed. Then in April, the battalion heard that Major-Gen Salmon, the Divisional Commander, had been killed in an air crash on his way to Egypt. In May, the battalion was brought up to an expanded war establishment. Shortly thereafter they departed for Scotland for advanced amphibious training. Hardening exercises and practice landings were followed by larger exercises carried out from the transport *Llangibby Castle*. They disembarked for a three week period of mountain training, then on 14 June again boarded the *Llangibby Castle*. Other major exercises followed. The ship returned to the Clyde and this time the unit did not disembark. On the evening of 28 June they sailed out of the river. Two days later, as they headed south, the admiral in command of the convoy announced that they they were bound for the Mediterranean.

On 1 July briefings for the invasion of Sicily began. A vast amount of information had been provided for the battalion in the form of maps, air photographs, terrain models and so on. In addition there were geographic and geological surveys and the complex instructions for unloading and landing. Officers grimly waded into the task of digesting the material. It was difficult to believe that so much could be committed to memory in such a short time.

The intelligence reports discounted the fighting qualities of the 200,000 Italian troops in Sicily but were much more respectful

about the two German divisions located in the island. The 1st
Canadian Division, commanded by Major-Gen G. G. Simonds,
was to land on the south coast of Sicily on the left of the British
Eighth Army.

On 4 July the convoy carrying the division passed Gibraltar and
moved along the north coast of Africa. On the 9th, when it turned
to the north to approach around Malta there were high winds and
the sea was rough. For a time the landings that night appeared to
be in jeopardy but the weather calmed. Shortly after midnight the
assaulting companies boarded their heaving landing-craft and
headed for shore. No one had told the assaulting troops that up to
30% casualties were expected in the landings but they anticipated
no picnic. As they approached the beach, they could see machine-
gun tracer and the flash of exploding grenades, but no hail of fire
met them on the beach.

In a matter of hours the coastal defences were breached and the
battalion had begun the advance inland. The Italian defenders had
had no stomach for a fight.

For the next few days, the battalion advanced northwards,
through the heat and dust, encountering only nominal resistance from
the defending forces. After more than a month of enforced inactivity
on board ship, the troops found the long marches exhausting. Lack
of rest bothered them far more than the enemy did. The number of
prisoners became embarrassing.

A week after the landings the 2nd Brigade had marched more
than halfway across Sicily and it was then that they met the
Germans. For four more days they were initiated into the frustrations of driving-in the highly competent rearguards of Panzer
Grenadiers in mountainous country.

The bastion of the German defences was Mount Etna on the
east coast of the island. Here they blocked the main body of the
Eighth Army advancing toward Messina, the nearest point to the
Italian mainland. The Canadians, moving northwards in the centre
of Sicily, were ordered to capture the town of Leonforte and there
turn east towards Mount Etna, taking its defences from the flank.
Leonforte was the hinge. Every step which the Canadians took to
the east of it weakened the enemy defences. From now on the going
would be tougher.

Leonforte is a typical Italian hill-town, dominating the surrounding countryside. The only approach from the south is by a switch-back road, which angles down the face of a ravine, crosses it by a narrow bridge, then climbs the opposite side to the town's gates. Its entire length was in full view of the defenders who had, of course, blown the bridge.

During the evening of 21 July the Edmonton Regiment fought their way into the town. The enemy mounted a powerful counter-attack and before long all communications with the Edmontons broke down. In the meantime, engineers of the 3rd Field Company worked under heavy fire to replace the blown bridge. All night, the sound of firing came from Leonforte, where the Germans closed in on the isolated battalion. Early in the morning, the bridge was completed and the brigade commander ordered C Company, PPCLI, four tanks of the Three Rivers Regiment and a troop of anti-tank guns to cross the bridge and open a path to the Edmontons.

The infantry were mounted on the tanks and guns, some even sitting astride the barrels. At break-neck speed they crossed the bridge and raced up the hill into Leonforte. The column was swept by fire but only one man was hit before they burst into the German positions by the gates. Soon Capt R. C. Coleman's company was involved in street fighting, as they fought their way forward into the town. By ten o'clock they had reached the surrounded headquarters of the Edmonton Regiment. As they battled on toward the northern outskirts, fighting grew in intensity. Tanks fought each other at ten yards range, and anti-tank guns on both sides caused heavy casualties. C Company seized the railway station on the northern side of Leonforte where they were twice counter-attacked. By afternoon the town was clear. The Germans on the high ground to the east and west still commanded its approaches and A and B Companies were ordered to take the positions. By 5.30 that afternoon they had done so.

The last phase of the battle developed into a series of small engagements by platoons and sections, which showed that the fighting qualities of the Regiment were as high as ever. In the words of the official Canadian History, 'Among the many deeds of bravery performed that day in and about the hard-won town (altogether twenty-one awards were made for the Leonforte engagement) none was more spectacular than that of Pte S. J. Cousins, a member of A Company of the Patricias. During the company's assault on the height referred to above the leading platoons were halted by the intensity of fire coming from two enemy machine gun posts on the objective. While they were reorganizing, Cousins, accompanied by an NCO, on his own initiative advanced against the German positions. One hundred and fifty yards from the crest, Cousins' companion fell under the hail of bullets which swept the slope. Despite the fact that further progress appeared to be utter suicide to the men of his company who were watching this gallant soldier, he then, with complete disregard for his own life, rose to his feet in full view of the enemy and, carrying his Bren gun boldly, charged the enemy posts. This resolute action so demoralized the enemy that he was able to close within less than fifty yards of their positions. Then, firing from the hip, he killed or wounded the German machine gunners, silencing both posts. A Company took and successfully held the ridge; but unfortunately Private Cousins was killed later in the afternoon by a direct hit. He was subsequently Mentioned in Dispatches.'

There was no longer any doubt – the Patricias were back at war again.

The Canadian advance continued to the east. The PPCLI were again engaged in the capture of Agira, and on the approaches to Monte Seggio. The German defences were worn down, then collapsed. When the campaign in Sicily ended, the 1st Canadian Division was in reserve preparing to cross to the mainland of Italy.

Chapter 6
The Professional Amateurs

THE battalion which rested at Militello before crossing to Italy had a new and distinctive character of its own. Few of the old 'PF'ers' were left. The years of training in Britain followed by the brief Sicilian campaign had changed the volunteers of 1939 into skilled and experienced soldiers. In addition to being trained as basic infantrymen, the men of the rifle companies were qualified as drivers, signallers, mortar men and anti-tank gunners. Privates were qualified as corporals. They had experienced in training almost every type of operation which they were likely to meet. Home ties had drawn thinner with the years abroad, and more and more the men's lives centred on the Regiment. They had become professionals in everything but name.

Veterans looking back at the Italian campaign recall that for the first months men coming to the Patricias as replacements for battle casualties were also well-trained. But as preparations progressed for the cross-channel operations in 1944, their quality diminished and there were seldom enough to bring the unit up to strength. In the fall and winter of 1944, many Canadians looked upon Italy as the 'forgotten theatre', a side show to north-west Europe.

From the beginning the Patricias found Italy a land of contrasts which they little understood. They enjoyed the cheerful peasants of the South and were appalled by the dirt in which they lived, felt pity for the poor and were revolted by the excesses of wealth, admired the beauty of the country and cursed the heat and the dust, the cold and the mud. They were glad to leave in 1945, but grumbled because they did so before the war there had ended.

Looking back at the fighting in Sicily, men realized that it had been much easier than they had expected. The same was to be true of the first few weeks in Italy.

During the morning of 4 September, 1943, the Patricias, now

under the command of Lt-Col C. B. Ware, crossed from San Alessio in Sicily to Reggio Calabria. In the next sixteen days they advanced over 450 miles. The 3rd Canadian Brigade, which had crossed the Straits of Messina first, had taken all the objectives of the 1st Canadian Division. The Patricias were ordered to follow in their wake up the centre of the Calabrian Peninsula. There followed four days of wearying marches along poor secondary roads. Where these lay along the side of a hill the bridges were blown over every water-course, soon separating the marching troops from their transport. Where they crossed the grain of the country, marching became a tedious succession of steep climbs and descents. On 8 September the battalion learned of the Italian surrender. The Canadians were now brought down from the hills and were relieved to continue their advance in transport along the coastal road. After a welcome four-day halt by the sea at Catanzaro, the Patricias motored half-way along the foot of Italy, then turned north-west to Potenza. The rapid advance of the Canadians, with the 5th British Division on their left, had prevented the Germans from concentrating all their forces against the Salerno bridgehead. With their arrival in force at Potenza, the enemy started to withdraw and the Allies began their long advance up the boot.

So far the Patricias had met little to hold up their advance except cratered roads and demolished bridges. From now on the going became slower as the Germans began to demonstrate their skill in the withdrawal. Every practical line of advance was sown with mines. Machine guns were sited to cut down soldiers who attempted to lift them. Mortars were trained on nearby ditches or depressions, where cover might be found. The advance could not continue until first these hampering weapons and then the mines had been cleared from the way. An attack would be mounted, often by a laborious route around the flank, only to find that the Germans had withdrawn a few hundred yards further and the process had to be repeated.

During the next four days battalion patrols worked 30 miles north of Potenza and secured the towns of Atella and Melfi. Some-times the battalion had as many as nine patrols out at once, searching for the enemy in the hills.

The Canadian Division had now been directed on Campobasso to the north-west. The morning of 1 October found the Regiment in a concentration area near Troia, preparing to cross the 40 miles of rough table land to the objective. Again there were few tracks and these were dominated by the surrounding hills, but now it was possible to move across country. For almost two weeks the 2nd Brigade worked forward in the direction of Campobasso. Several times the Patricias were ordered to mount battalion attacks against positions believed to be strongly held by the enemy only to find that he had withdrawn. There were brushes with German tanks and infantry, neither side suffering many casualties. On 14 October, Campobasso was occupied by the Royal Canadian Regiment without a fight. Beyond lay the Biferno River where the enemy might be expected to make a stand.

For a week the Desert Air Force softened up villages and other enemy positions west of the river. On the night of 22/23 October the Loyal Edmonton Regiment crossed the Biferno and seized the village which was their objective. They were promptly counter-attacked by tanks. The Patricias were to cross the river later in the day and seize the village of Spinetti. A patrol reconnoitring their forming-up area was pinned down by shell-fire. A real battle seemed to be in prospect for a change, but again there was little resistance. For two days the battalion patrolled beyond the objective, one penetrating 15 miles into the wooded hills to the west to bring out twenty-one British, South African and Indian escaped prisoners of war. The scouts and snipers engaged some 60 of the enemy in Frosolone, but next day when a fighting patrol came to clear the village, it was empty.

On 27 October the Patricias were relieved and moved into billets in Busso where they remained for a month of rest, leave and training. They had worked hard but had suffered little. Some among them felt that because there had been so little fighting the Army should by now have been far farther north in Italy than it was. Often the fighting troops had been unable to advance because their supporting arms and administrative services had been unable to keep up. In volume III of the regimental history, Col G. R. Stevens points out that the problem of driving the Germans head-long up Italy was more one for the sapper than for the infantryman. The engineers who were there had done as much as men could do, 'but it was not as much as could have been done if the physical problems of advancing through a mountainous peninsula had been more accurately evaluated before the invasion had been launched'.

By November, the Allies had occupied a third of the country. While the Canadians rested and enjoyed the unaccustomed delights of the Divisional leave centre at Campobasso, the 5th and 78th British Divisions were fighting a very different war as they advanced up the east coast. By now there was no question but that the Germans would stand and fight and the British formations were suffering heavy casualties. At the beginning of December the Patricias moved out of their comfortable billets, moved down to the coast road and joined the crawling stream of traffic which took them slowly forward to the Sangro River. They bivouacked four miles to the north. The biting cold winds and incessant rain of the Italian winter had begun and the enemy were present in force. On the evening of 4 December, the Patricias relieved the 6th Royal Iniskilling Fusiliers on the southern edge of the Moro valley. Many look back on that date as the beginning of the serious war.

The enemy's main defensive position lay between the river and the lateral road that ran from the heavily fortified town of Orsogna on the edge of the Maiella mountains, north-east to the bastion of Ortona on the coast. The Canadian plan was to breach the centre of the enemy defences and then exploit to the sea at Ortona. The Patricias were to take the village of Villa Rogatti, which dominated a crossing site on the Moro on the left of the divisional advance. It was held by the 200th Panzer Grenadier Regiment of the 9th German Infantry Division. Little was known of their dispositions, but patrols reported them to be holding posts around the outskirts of the village with a central garrison inside. They had seen traffic moving between Rogatti and the main German defences to the rear, thus it would be possible for the enemy to counter-attack with armour if their positions were lost.

The Patricias were to be supported by a squadron of the 44th Royal Tank Regiment. On the night of 5 December the rifle companies moved into their forming-up places and at midnight B Company advanced silently across the stream and felt its way toward the village. German sentries opened fire and soon machine guns were firing from the village. B Company rushed the outposts and began to work into the town. Surprise had been so complete that some German prisoners were taken in their beds. The advance now slowed as the rifle platoons cleared the enemy from the southern part of the town. A Company, which was following, now moved towards the northern part of the village, clearing the enemy from a small gully which intervened. By first light the PPCLI were firmly in control of Villa Rogatti. Enemy artillery and mortar fire on the village began to increase in intensity. The German infantry in the nearby olive groves swept the outskirts with machine and rifle fire. It was obvious that the enemy would soon counter-attack and supplies and ammunition were running low.

The tanks which were to support the Patricias were working forward across the Moro but their advance was delayed by the difficult going. For two hours, A Company had been under heavy fire as infantry of the 200th Panzer Grenadier Regiment closed in on them through the mist. Just as the Germans were about to charge, the first of the British tanks arrived on the scene. The seemingly inexhaustible stream of fire from their machine guns was music to the ears of the hard-pressed Patricias. As the Germans fell back pack mules arrived with ammunition. The tanks pulled back into hull-down positions and the battalion prepared to renew its advance, but were ordered by Brigade to consolidate where they were.

At half-past two the Panzer Grenadiers attacked again, supported by nine tanks of the 26th Panzer Regiment. This time it was B Company who met them. Almost at once three of the enemy tanks were knocked out. In two groups, the enemy drove forward against the flanks of the Patricia company. The battle continued for more than two hours. Five times the Germans came forward and were beaten back by the fire of the Patricias and 44 RTR. Finally it was

15. *A section of the PPCLI engages German transport during the advance towards Enna, Sicily, 1943.*

16. *Crossing the Moro River at Villa Rogatti, Italy, December, 1943.*

17. *Major J. E. Leach, 'A' Company Commander briefs his FOO and signaller outside Ortona, January, 1944.*

18. *Patricias landing on the west bank of the Ijssel, 11 April, 1945.*

over. Five German tanks had been destroyed, 40 prisoners captured and more than 100 of the enemy had been killed. An unexpected tribute to the defenders was found in the war diary of the 26th Panzer Division which spoke of the 'excellent fire discipline of the enemy who let our tanks approach within 50 metres and then destroyed them'. As night fell the battalion regrouped and stretcher bearers began the long two-mile carry back to the dressing station with the wounded. The losses had been the heaviest so far in a day's fighting.

Twenty-four hours later the Patricias were relieved by troops of the 21st Indian Brigade and moved back to their start line to prepare for another phase in the attack.

The Canadian plan was to move north across the Orsogna – Ortona road, then turn to drive north-east along it to the sea. Between them and the road lay a long narrow ravine whose steep sides made a perfect tank obstacle. The Germans seized upon it as the most easily defensible feature to block the allied advance. It was bridged where a road leading north from the Moro through San Leonardo crossed it. The Loyal Edmonton Regiment were to secure the junction of this road with the Ortona – Orsogna highway 300 yards beyond. This objective was given the code name 'Cider', the ravine was known simply as 'the Gully'. When the attack of the Edmontons was successful, the Patricias were to advance south of the Gully in the direction of the sea, along a spur known as Vino Ridge. Once secured, they would dominate the southern outskirts of Ortona.

The strength of the Gully's defences was completely unexpected and they brought the Edmontons' attack to a halt. The German defensive fire caught the PPCLI both in San Leonardo and as they moved up to the position from which they would attack. Three company commanders were among the casualties. Col Ware received a report that the Edmontons had secured 'Cider' and ordered the Patricias to advance. When he learned that the report was a mistake it was too late to stop the attack. The battalion's left flank was exposed to the Gully and little progress was made that afternoon.

The following day the Patricias were ordered to strike out further along Vino Ridge toward the coast. Supported by tanks of the Calgary Regiment, they fought their way forward through positions obstinately defended by the Germans. Mines and booby traps infested the vineyards and olive groves. Late in the afternoon they beat off a counter-attack and when darkness fell they had reached the edge of the Gully on the right of the Edmontons. Further attacks on 13 and 14 December gained the Regiment nothing but casualties. By the 15th the battalion only had enough men to operate three under-strength rifle companies, but morale was high. Col Ware declined offers of wire and mines to protect his front. He commented that he did not need wire and as for mines, the enemy had already laid them.

But a crack had been found in the enemy defences. On the left flank of the division the Royal 22e Regiment had outflanked the head of the Gully and swept along the main road to seize Casa Berardi, a prominent white house in the centre of the division's front. Four days later a major assault exploited their success and secured the crossings of the Gully. On 19 December the Patricias advanced along Vino Ridge to within 600 yards of the outskirts of Ortona.

The 2nd Canadian Infantry Brigade now had the task of clearing Heidrich's paratroopers from the town. The PPCLI were to provide a firm base for the operation while the Loyal Edmonton Regiment and the Seaforth Highlanders of Canada battled through the streets. Few can have expected the struggle for the little Adriatic city to have been so long and bitter. For seven days the Canadians fought their way through it in some of the most ferocious fighting of the war. Col Ware and his company commanders made frequent visits to the battalions in the city expecting at any time to be committed to the struggle. In the evening of the 27th, they moved in to take up the battle from the Edmontons but in the morning the enemy was gone.

The battalion advanced beyond Ortona and remained there until they were relieved on 30 December. They had been unable to pay more than lip service to Christmas but the New Year was celebrated in style.

For two weeks the battalion remained in Ortona, then moved out once more to a position on the northern outskirts. Winter had halted the 8th Army's advance and there followed six weeks of patrolling. The weather was foul, with wet snow and cold winds. The Germans were alert and aggressive, ingenious in their use of mines and booby traps. Patrols were usually cold and wet but never dull.

At the end of February the Patricias left Ortona and two weeks later relieved the Perth Regiment near Crecchio, five miles inland from their last position. Again their time was spent in patrolling, but as the weather improved this became a less unattractive activity and efforts to harass the enemy were increased. Patrols were out every night and each had its adventure, often amusing to report.

The town of Crecchio was occupied by the Germans. To help them celebrate Hitler's birthday, Sgt W. L. MacKay, another sniper sergeant in the tradition of the redoubtable Christie, with one scout, 'holed up' in a church tower in the town. The streets were decorated with Swastika flags. As the garrison began their Nazi tribal rite with the ringing of church bells and singing, the Patricias added their contribution of mortar salvoes. MacKay and his companion returned the following evening highly delighted with the performance.

On 23 April the battalion was relieved by troops of the 10th Indian Division and moved to a rest area south of Campobasso. It was obvious to all that they were to take part in the advance on Rome. As the regimental history notes, 'the Patricias had been at rest in Guardiaregia for a week, when high commanders began to arrive – harbingers of battle as certain as the first robin is of spring'. On 8 May, the anniversary of Frezenberg, the battalion began infantry tank training with the North Irish Horse. It was the beginning of a much-valued association between the two regiments. On the 12th they began to move toward the new battlefield by the Appian Way, the historic road which runs from Naples to Rome. Almost half-way between those two cities, the Liri valley, through which ran the main road and rail lines, was blocked by two formidable German defensive lines anchored on Monte Casino. The assault on the first, the Gustav line, had begun when the Patricias started to move. Breaching the second, the Hitler line, was to be their task.

On the 16th they were called forward and the following day bivouacked under direct observation from Monte Casino. All day they were under mortar, machine gun and artillery fire and that night suffered casualties from a bombing and machine gun attack from the air. The Gustav line had been breached and on the 18th Monte Casino was taken. For four more days preparations were made for the attack on the Hitler line. Orders for the assault were changed at least four times by higher headquarters and it was not until noon on 22 May that the Patricias were given their final orders for the assault the next morning.

They were to breach the Hitler line on the extreme right of the divisions' assault, moving parallel to the Forme D'Aquino, a small stream. Beyond it, overlooking their flank, was the heavily defended town of Aquino. The approaches to the enemy wire lay through scrub oak and undergrowth.

At 6 o'clock in the morning of the 23rd, A and C Companies advanced behind a thunderous barrage toward the Hitler line. B Company followed with the task of mopping up.

Immediately, the enemy opened a devastating defensive fire from concealed pill-boxes and from Aquino on the flank. Col Ware received a report that A Company had reached the wire. Then nothing more was heard. All attempts to communicate by liaison officers and runner failed and supporting arms could not get forward through the intense enemy fire. The North Irish Horse attempting to help the Regiment forward were restricted in their movement by the Forme D'Aquino on the right and by deep laid mines which had defied detection. They were caught in a trap of concealed self-propelled guns and twenty-five of their tanks were destroyed that day.

So many casualties occurred in such a short time that it was difficult to piece together the full story of the battle. Platoons disappeared from the sight of their company commanders and were lost. Every man accompanying Major W. de N. Watson, commanding A Company, was a casualty. Hoping to find his platoons on the objective he pressed on alone. There was no trace of his men and the enemy were there in strength. By that time he had been wounded twice. He managed to evade capture and finally settled down in a 'large and quite comfortable shell hole'. During the night he once more went forward to the objective hoping that it might now have been taken. The enemy were still there. The next day he lay concealed and the following morning, the War Diary records, 'Major Watson was located in a shell hole, near an 88 mm gun, suffering from a wound in one arm, a piece of his helmet and a Schmeisser bullet in his forehead, and a tremendous appetite'.

Two of the Patricias company commanders who were fast friends were noted for their taciturnity. Major C. M. McDougall, on discovering Watson greeted him with 'Hello, Bucko'. Watson looked up and replied, 'Oh, hello Colin'. An eye witness swears that this was their complete conversation.

Many wounded Patricias were found well beyond the wire and more than thirty unwounded men of the assaulting companies were later found to have gone to ground on the objective or beyond.

On the left, the Seaforth Highlanders had penetrated to the objective, but their assaulting companies were wiped out. The Edmontons, attempting to pass through the Patricias, failed to get beyond the wire. The casualties of the 2nd Brigade were the highest that day that a brigade suffered in the Italian campaign. On the left, however, the attack by the 1st Brigade had been successful and on the 29th the Patricias were again on the move following up the advance. Some 20 miles to the north-west, at Frosinone, after some brushes with enemy rearguards, the battle ended for the Patricias. U.S. troops advancing from Anzio were within sight of Rome and the 1st Canadian Corps went into reserve. There followed almost two months of rest and training south-east of Casino. At the end of June, Col Ware left and was replaced by his second-in-command, Major D. H. Rosser.

The next task for the Canadian Corps would be the breaking of the Gothic line on the opposite coast of Italy – a new position which the Germans had prepared some 200 miles north of those from which they had just been driven. But first, in order to deceive them as to where the attack would fall, the 1st Canadian Division went into the line south of the Arno at Florence. For three days the Patricias patrolled against the enemy and repulsed one brisk attack. There was no doubt that they had been identified by the veterans of the 4th Parachute Division who opposed them. On 8 August they were relieved by Indian troops and, removing all badges and signs on their vehicles, moved to a training area south of the line. Ten days later they crossed the Apennines and bivouacked south of the new battle area.

When they attacked on the evening of 25 August the men braced themselves for the kind of opposition which they had met three months earlier in the Liri valley. Instead it was a walk-over. On the way to their first objective, closely following the heavy and accurate barrage, the only casualties were three men injured by mines. The Canadians had attacked before they were expected and in the least likely area. Opposition increased but in only two days the country between the Metauro River and the Foglia was cleared. Col Rosser went down with malaria and Major R. P. Clark took command.

The next phase in the battle promised to be more costly. Beyond the Foglia River strong enemy defences had been identified. Machine-gun cupolas at ground level covered mine fields which lay across every line of approach. An anti-tank ditch covered the front but wire obstacles appeared to be incomplete. The Patricias were to form the centre of the three battalion front on which the 1st Corps would attack. The ruins of the village of Osteria Nuova, which lay about a mile beyond the river, were the Regiment's first objective. Again, surprisingly, the battalion met with little opposition as they crossed the Foglia and moved beyond it. B Company negotiated a mine field walking in single file. Only three men were lost in this hazardous episode.

The West Nova Scotia Regiment on the right had been held up by resistance of a very different order. British tanks joined the Patricias and, together with A Company, took from its flank the strong point which was delaying the eastern Regiment. In the next two days the Patricias drove forward until they were halted at Gradara, close to the sea. The Gothic line had been broken.

There followed two weeks in reserve in Cattolica, during which Col Rosser returned from hospital. The 1st Canadian Corps was continuing the advance and had crossed the Marano River, driving up the coast toward the next line of German defences which ran inland from the city of Rimini.

On 16 September, as the Patricias prepared to enter the battle, battalion headquarters was heavily shelled and Col Rosser was wounded. The second-in-command, Major R. P. Clark, was promoted to succeed him.

The approach to the main defences of the Rimini line, lying along the Ausa River, was blocked by a low but dominating ridge surmounted by the town of San Martino. Several successive Canadian attempts to capture it had failed. The Patricias were ordered to relieve the Royal 22e Regiment at the southern extremity of this feature and begin its isolation by infiltrating round its western flank. Patrols were to be despatched to the rear and if a soft spot was found, the battalion was to advance to the river.

On the night of the 16th the operation began. Attempts to push patrols forward failed when they encountered the enemy in strength within 200 yards. Early next morning C Company observed a strong enemy force preparing to attack, but drove them off with the aid of a troop of tanks of the 145th Regiment, RAC. Slowly the companies worked forward in an attempt to expand the gap toward the river. Casualties from shelling were heavy.

Early next morning the battalion attacked toward the line of the river 2,000 yards ahead. By 8 o'clock, half of the strength of the rifle companies were casualties. Two hours later the remaining sixty men dug in within 200 yards of their objective. The movement had made San Martino untenable. The enemy withdrew leaving the way open for an attack on San Fortunato, the last bastion which protected Rimini. Twenty-four hours later it fell to a brilliant attack by the Seaforths, Edmontons and Vingt-Deuxs.

Next morning the Patricias were ordered to exploit to the Corps objective which was the next river line, the Marecchia. That afternoon they advanced, supported by tanks of the 12th Royal Tank Regiment. Half way to the objective their way was blocked at the village of Montecello by a battle group with five or six Tiger tanks. Air strikes and artillery were ineffective. The battalion's anti-tank guns and supporting tanks were unable to cross the steep and greasy slopes of the San Fortunato ridge. To make matters worse, radio communications were bad. Col Clark decided to by-pass the enemy force and by early next morning A Company had crossed the Marecchia River and reached the Emilian Way. The enemy south of the river melted away. B Company crossed and turned to the right to exploit toward Rimini and the remaining rifle companies joined A Company in the bridgehead. During the night the battalion position was shelled and C Company lost its third company commander killed in the battle. B Company, after clearing machine gun posts from their way, and brushing against a strong enemy force of infantry and tanks reached Celle on the coastal highway. Their strength was down to forty. There they were taken under command by the 22nd New Zealand Motor Battalion and the battle was over.

On 23 September the PPCLI marched back to billets in Cattolica. For a few days they enjoyed themselves on the beaches, then began to prepare for the next phase of operations which were to take place in the flat plains of the Romagna. This vast reclaimed swamp promised them a taste of the water-logged conditions their fathers had known in Flanders.

The Patricias joined the advance into the Lombardy plain when, on 19 October, they struck out from the newly-won bridgehead over the Pisciatello River toward the Savio River north of Cesena. By the next morning two companies were in position near the river at Martorano and the battalion prepared for an opposed crossing. That night the assault went in. So heavy was the enemy defensive fire that only one platoon of A Company succeeded in crossing. Major E. W. Cutbill, the company commander, arrived to find that his total force was seventeen men. They headed for the objective. After they had cleared an outpost from their path, he despatched an NCO back across the Savio to brief the CO on the situation and bring over a radio and reinforcements. At 4 am he returned with eighteen men and orders to hold on.

Col Clark was now ordered not to attempt to expand the bridgehead further. The Loyal Edmonton Regiment and the Seaforths would cross on a two battalion front next evening.

All day Cutbill and his little force were under heavy fire. Despite casualties and shortages of ammunition they held their position against enemy counter attacks and even sent fighting patrols to silence the more troublesome German positions. At about 8 pm, they were joined in their position by a company of the Seaforths and by midnight the western bank of the Savio was held to a depth of 500 yards.

Twenty-four hours later D Company assaulted across the river under command of the West Nova Scotia Regiment in an attempt to widen the bridgehead. At first light they were counter-attacked by enemy tanks which, without their support weapons, they were unable to stop. One platoon lay low while the Panzers swept past them. One of the companies of the West Nova Scotia Regiment who accompanied them was caught by German infantry and tanks before they could gain a foothold and the commanding officer ordered them to withdraw. There was no communication with the Patricia platoons. Eventually, however, most made their way back.

During a lull in the fighting an officer employed at a very high headquarters came forward to visit his old company. He commented later that there is always an awareness of risk as one goes forward from the rear toward the battle area, from a zone which is comparatively immune from attack into one where shells fall, then from it forward to the target area of enemy mortars, bombs and bullets. Serving at an Army Headquarters, he experienced the sensation even when he visited one of the forward divisional headquarters. He confessed to being contemptuous of himself in finding this trace of what he took to be fear in his make-up. The final humiliation came when he came upon D Company resting. There was only one man left with it whom he recognized and he was sitting quietly swearing to himself in a ditch. The officer slid down beside him, offered a cigarette and asked what was bothering him, 'It's this bloody war, sir, and the bloody way they treat this bloody platoon. Next time, I'm going to get one of those cushy jobs back at company headquarters!'

The Germans were finally forced out of their positions when they were in danger of being out-flanked from the south, and the three battalions of 2nd Brigade pushed out patrols. But before contact was made again, the Canadians were ordered into reserve. On 26 October the battalion was relieved by the 12th Lancers who were not overly pleased at being taken from their tanks to serve as infantry.

For a month the battalion rested at Riccione. From 9 to 18 December they were employed in securing the rear of the formations engaged in crossing yet further of the Italian river lines, then in clearing the left flank of the Division for about a mile to the Naviglio Canal at Bagnacavallo. It was a period of fighting patrols and ambushes in which the Patricias soon established their superiority over the enemy.

On the night of the 14th the Patricias moved over the Naviglio Canal into the bridgehead established by the Edmontons and Seaforths and the three battalions drove to expand it in preparation for a break-out. They were relieved by the Carleton and York Regiment on the 16th and three days later again crossed the Canal to the north and attacked to secure the line of the River Munio. After three days of heavy fighting they did so and, moving south, cleared its banks as far as Bagnacavallo.

There followed a lull which lasted until well after Christmas during which a new assault was prepared to establish the 1st Canadian Corps along the line of the River Senio which would be their 'winter line'.

The Patricias' part was to cross the Naviglio Canal once more and, with the Seaforths, isolate the German held town of Granarolo which the Edmontons would then clear. The operation went like clockwork. The barrage was accurate and easy to follow and troops were well-placed to meet enemy counter-attacks. The battalion's success, was matched by the Seaforths and when the Edmontons entered the town they met no resistance.

From now until the end of their war in Italy, the Patricias engaged in static warfare along the Senio, patrolling and raiding. As one remarked, 'If it had not been for the weather, we'd have enjoyed it'. There were many successes and one notable disaster. Two platoons of C Company raided a group of buildings on the Fosso Vecchio after a heavy artillery concentration. The enemy fled and as the Patricias entered the first of the buildings, a delayed charge brought it down on their heads. When others ran to dig them out, the enemy brought down a devastating mortar concentration. The action cost thirty-seven casualties.

For a few weeks the battalion was in reserve as a counter-attack force and then for two more were back on the Senio. Spring was in the air when they were relieved by the 5th Royal West Kents on 25 February. They embussed and began to move by easy stages across the Apennines to Pisa. On 12 March they embarked at Leghorn for France. 1st Canadian Corps was joining the major forces of the Army in north-west Europe.

When the Battalion landed at Marseilles and began the drive up the Rhone Valley toward Holland the men felt they were entering a new world of lush green beauty and cleanliness. The week which they spent moving by easy stages through Burgundy to the east of Paris, then by Cambrai to the suburbs of Brussels, and finally to the village of Boisschot, between Malines and Antwerp, had more of the atmosphere of a sightseeing trip than a military move. They were warmly welcomed in their new billets and for the first time since leaving Britain, many of the troops slept between clean white sheets.

The war in north-west Europe was reaching its final stages. The Allied Armies were closed up to the Rhine and the Americans had seized the crossing at Remagen. Two days after the Patricias arrived in Belgium, on 23 March, the 21st Army Group crossed the river and began the advance into Germany. 1st Canadian Corps from Italy was to clear the Germans from western Holland. As 2nd Canadian Corps drove north into Holland from the Rhine bridgehead the 1st Division would follow until they were in position along the Ijssel River, facing west.

The Patricias left Boisschot on 3 April with some regret. It had been a pleasant time of sports and not too arduous training. Old equipment had been replaced by new and many had spent a short leave in England. Above all, the local people were clean, smiling and friendly.

The men soon saw that they were heading back to battle. On the first night they bivouacked in the rain and mud of the Reichswald Forest. Everywhere lay the debris of battle and the towns were devastated. As they drove down the west bank of the Rhine toward the crossing at Wesel through the driving rain, they laughed at the military police signs warning that 'Dust draws shells'. On 9 April they moved into a concentration area at Baak, 4,000 yards from the Ijssel. Two days later they crossed the river in 'buffaloes', the tracked amphibians of the 4th Royal Tank Regiment. A tank and some well-positioned machine guns opposed the advance but the leading companies skillfully disposed of them all, the tank having been stopped and destroyed by an NCO of D Company with a PIAT.

It was almost 3 o'clock next morning, as B Company were moving into position on the perimeter of the bridgehead, when they heard enemy tanks moving toward them. A platoon moved swiftly into an ambush position along the road on which they approached. They allowed the three enemy tanks and a company of infantry which followed to pass, then opened fire on their rear. Several wheeled vehicles and 80 prisoners were captured in a wild melée. The tanks with about a platoon of infantry continued on their way. D Company fired on them as they crossed their front, but the column headed stolidly on until it reached A Company. The tanks were engaged by PIATS; the German infantry attacked the PIAT sections and the Patricia riflemen waylaid the German infantry. All the tanks were destroyed and within an hour the only German survivors were prisoners.

At 5 am on 13 April the Patricias advanced out of the bridgehead towards the west, then, on the 15th, swung south in the direction of Arnhem. A patrol bicycling down the road met troops of the 49th British Division advancing to meet them. The Canadians and

British now turned and for the next three days cleared the country to the west.

The Germans were trapped. To avoid unnecessary hardship to the Dutch population and further destruction of the country Head-quarters of 21st Army Group deliberately slowed the advance. Action was confined to brushes with enemy patrols in which many prisoners were taken by the battalion. On 27 April an ambush was laid for an enemy group five miles west of Barneveld. Several Germans were killed and five were taken prisoner. In it the PPCLI fired their last shots of the Second World War.

The Patricias' area included the village of Achterveld and thus they found themselves involved in the surrender of the German Forces in the Netherlands. On 28 April German emissaries met Major-General de Guingand, Field-Marshal Montgomery's Chief of Staff, and other Allied officers in the village school house. When it was found that the enemy officers had no power to act they were sent away. Another meeting with General Eisenhower's Chief of Staff, Lt-Gen Bedell Smith was fixed for two days later. Prince Bernhard of the Netherlands was present and the Germans included Seyss-Inquart and the Chief of the enemy forces in the Netherlands. It was agreed that the armies would stand fast and that convoys of food would be moved in to feed the starving Dutch population. A period of watchful waiting ensued until, on 5 May, the Germans in northern Europe surrendered to Field-Marshal Montgomery on Lunenberg Heath.

For the Patricias it seemed that the war had ground slowly to a halt. As on 11 November, 1918, there was no surge of joy, no celebrations. There could be no relaxation of routine, for the Canadians had another task to perform – the occupation of western Holland and the evacuation of German troops from the country. The Patricias were to be responsible for the Haarlem area, immediately west of Amsterdam.

At dawn on 7 May Col Clark, with a small reconnaissance party, set out to meet the German commanders. The enemy, fully armed and alert, were still manning their defences and seemed surprised to see the Allied vehicles. Col Clark reported, 'Upon arriving at

Amsterdam early in the morning, the city appeared to be deserted, but continuing down the main street, the people suddenly recognized an Allied vehicle. There were a few shouts, then heads began to pop out of windows. Before we got to the end of this long main street, it seemed as though the whole population of the city was blocking our path. It took us a considerable time to push through to meet the German commanders in the Haarlem area.

'From all appearances, no Allied soldiers had been along this main road from the south until my small party arrived.'

It seems likely that the Patricias were the first Allies to enter Amsterdam. Next day, the 30th anniversary of Frezenberg, the Regiment motored to their new area. It was a triumphal entry. All along the route buildings were decked with flags and the roads were lined with cheering Dutch people. When they reached Amsterdam the convoy was literally engulfed as the crowds brought it to a halt and people climbed on the vehicles to embrace the soldiers. An equally warm welcome greeted them at Haarlem, but there they were immediately almost swamped with work, shoring up the struggling civilian administration and disarming and repatriating the German forces. They even had to protect enemy soldiers and collaborators from the violent elements in the Dutch Resistance Movement.

The war with Japan was still to be ended and the Canadian Government was readying a force to take part in the final invasion of that country. Almost 160 officers and men of the battalion volunteered to join it. Others agreed to remain in the Army of Occupation. Within weeks these had left the battalion, included among them, Col Clark. As the PPCLI would be one of the first units to return to Canada their places were taken by men from other units who had had long service overseas. On 9 September the battalion crossed from Ostend to Dover, then moved to a repatriation camp on Cobham Common, near Esher. There the Colonel-in-Chief reviewed her wartime battalion for the last time.

On 25 September they sailed from Southampton on the liner *Ile de France* for Halifax. From there two trains took them to Winnipeg. On the way the men were given leave passes for thirty days and told to report back at the end of it for demobilization. A huge crowd had assembled to meet them at the station. There was no attempt at formality. The battalion simply disappeared into the arms of its welcomers.

A final ceremony to mark the disbandment of the wartime battalion was held on 8 November in the Civic Auditorium in Winnipeg. For the Patricias the war was officially over.

Chapter 7
The Regular Soldiers

U NTIL the war in Europe ended Canada had been able to do little about her other major enemy, Japan. Japanese forces had overwhelmed two Canadian battalions in Hong Kong and had for a time threatened the West Coast. It had somehow seemed more natural for Canadian forces to be involved in Europe than in the Far East, but in 1945, it was obvious to all that Canada must play out her role as a Pacific country.

A Canadian Army Pacific Force was raised to take part in the invasion of Japan. It was to be organized along American lines, and was to serve under United States command. On 1 June it was announced that one of the battalions would be designated 'Princess Patricia's Canadian Light Infantry' and would be commanded by Lt-Col P. W. Strickland, DSO, ED, formerly CO of the Highland Light Infantry of Canada. It began to assemble towards the end of June at Camp Shilo, east of Brandon, Manitoba. A month later it moved to Camp MacDonald, near Portage le Prairie, where officers and men began to learn the mysteries of US Army organization and military procedures. On 15 August, however, the Japanese Emperor broadcast his unconditional surrender. The Pacific Force as such was no longer required, and on 1 September, it was disbanded.

When the First World War ended few men thought that war on a major scale would ever be seen again. In 1945, while the Axis powers had been more devastatingly crushed than the vanquished of 1918, men could not be so confident about the future peace of the world. Nor could Canada be sure that, if war came again, she would have a choice of being involved or not.

One thing seemed certain – never again could her forces be neglected as they had been between the wars. But deciding on their size and shape was another matter. It would take time to decide what she needed. In the meantime the old PF'ers and those who thought that they would like to make a career of soldiering were to be held in a new 'interim force' until the pattern of the postwar army was decided. On 2 September, 1945, the former Pacific Force battalion became the 2nd Battalion PPCLI, Interim Force. Col Strickland returned to civilian life and command passed to Major W. H. B. Matthews, who retained it until 3 January, 1946, when Lt-Col C. B. Ware, DSO, reported. On 17 January the battalion returned to Camp Shilo.

On 1 March the Government announced the post-war establishment of the forces. No longer would peacetime soldiers belong to the Militia. Officially there would be a Canadian Army, both Regular and Reserves. The Regular force would have 25,000 men, a full training and administrative base, with field units for each of the arms and services. Princess Patricia's Canadian Light Infantry (2nd Battalion was dropped from the title), at full war establishment would be part of it. The battalion would move to Fort Osborne Barracks, Winnipeg, early in May and a month later would proceed to a permanent station at Currie Barracks, Calgary, Alberta.

It was now possible to get down to work. Col Ware, who had experienced the frustrations of soldiering in the Permanent Force, realized how important it was to give the peacetime soldier a sense of purpose and direction. The improvement of overland communications to Alaska and the development of long range aircraft opened a possible threat to Canada's security from the North. It was time that the Army learned more about operating there. He obtained permission to take the battalion up the Alaska Highway.

With Lord Strathcona's Horse, the Patricias left for the Yukon on 16 August. The purpose was familiarization but much useful work was done in exploring possible river crossing sites, airfield defences and the like. The fishing and hunting were excellent. The exercise had the effect of knitting the unit closer together and of challenges of the North.

As the improved terms of service became known, recruiting

improved and many old soldiers came back to the Army. Through 1947 the strength of the battalion increased. In the winter there was ski training at Banff and arctic indoctrination courses at Fort Churchill. D Company and detachments of Headquarters Company trained in the Yukon, helped by arctic veterans of the Royal Canadian Mounted Police. In the summer the battalion ran a school for four months for 88 officer cadets of the Canadian Officer Training Corps and on 1 September they opened Camp Wainwright, a former prisoner of war camp, which was to become one of the country's major training areas. A month later Col Ware was replaced as commanding officer by Lt-Col N. M. Gemmell, DSO.

After the first World War, former members of the Regiment had formed Patricia Clubs in various parts of Canada and Britain. These had welcomed the veterans of the Second World War to their ranks. The Clubs were autonomous but all of them shared an interest in a common past and in the activities of the Regiment as a whole. In October, 1947, the Princess Patricia's Canadian Light Infantry Association was formed. Brig Hamilton Gault presided at the founding meeting in Calgary and took the salute at a ceremonial parade of the Regiment.

There was more arctic training that winter. Then, in June, 250 men of the Regiment were despatched to the lower Fraser Valley, in British Columbia, to fight disastrous floods. They prevented the waters from breaching over ten miles of dikes and saved much valuable farm land by their efforts.

It had become apparent to National Defence Headquarters that the only practicable way for the Army to engage an enemy force in the Arctic was to move by air. This led to the decision in 1948 to train a parachute battalion for such operations. The Patricias were selected. Since it was to involve a radical change in role, men were to be asked to volunteer for airborne training. On 8 August, the Vice Chief of the General Staff, Major-Gen C. C. Mann, CBE, DSO, visited the Regiment to brief them on their role and to obtain their reactions. Until he arrived, the unit did not know the purpose of his visit.

After announcing that the Patricias were to become an airborne unit, and explaining what its functions were to be, he asked each officer and man individually whether or not he would volunteer. Without exception, they did.

In October, Col Gemmell was succeeded in command by Lt-Col D. C. Cameron, DSO, ED, who had won great distinction commanding the Hastings and Prince Edward Regiment in Italy.

The PPCLI now formed part of the Mobile Striking Force, a battle group of infantry and supporting arms designed to deal with incursions into the Northland. Training the men to be parachutists turned out to be a much simpler process than finding the specialist kit which they needed, or the aircraft to carry them. In August, 1949, the first battalion-scale exercise, Exercise Eagle, was held in the Peace River district of northern Alberta and British Columbia. In the initial stages fire support would be provided from the air. The regimental history, speaking of the inadequacy of the air support, refers to the 'variegated fleet – 9 Mustangs, 16 Dakotas, 28 Harvard Trainers, 6 old Mitchell bombers, 3 North Stars, and a few miscellaneous crocks which might or might not stay in the air'. Everyone, including staff, learned a lot.

But the Patricias were not to be simply a parachute battalion. They also held all the kit, including carriers, heavy weapons and vehicles of a normal infantry unit. From 'Eagle' they went to Camp Wainwright for tactical training, which involved operations in armoured personnel carriers with tanks.

Much of the Regiment's adaptability was rooted in the high professional standards of their NCOs. From the time the Patricias were formed Commanding Officers have recognized that they are uniquely its hard core. They gave them responsibility and authority and treated them with the respect which their position deserved.

Watching over their training, their duties, their welfare and their social life have been a succession of formidable Regimental Sergeant Majors. Not only did they keep the NCOs and men up to the mark professionally, they were arbiters of regimental customs and traditions and of military conduct and deportment. They were held in universal awe and men of the Regiment delighted in telling stories which usually began 'So you think he's tough. You're lucky, you never met old . . .'

Typical of these was an incident in Currie Barracks where the manager of the Garrison Men's Canteen had begun to sell ice cream cones. This was tolerated provided they were consumed inside the building. But one day the RSM saw a young soldier walking toward the parade square carrying one in his hand. It was too much for his military sensibilities:

'What's that you've got?' he roared.

'An ice cream cone, Sir.'

'Get rid of it! No, don't throw it on the lawn, you idiot! Put it in your pocket!'

'Yes, Sir.'

'Now you've got a bulge in your uniform. Pat it flat!'

In January and February, 1950, the battalion took part in a major arctic exercise named 'Sweetbriar' with United States forces in the Yukon and Alaska. They were equipped with over-snow vehicles, but much movement was on foot. Temperatures were well below 0° Fahrenheit and at one point fell to −50°. In these conditions one company was dropped from Dakota aircraft to seize an airfield.

The Patricias were more experienced and better equipped for such operations than their US counterparts, who were quick and eager to learn from them. The exercise showed that the Canadian Army with its current equipment could operate effectively under such conditions. It provided a pattern for much of its future training.

In the spring there was another flood disaster, this time in Winnipeg. For most of a month the Regiment worked to save the city's suburbs. The annual Frezenberg Day celebrations were postponed until 17 June, after they had returned to Calgary. A few days later another event brought a change in the battalion's annual programme. On 25 June the Communists invaded South Korea.

Chapter 8

The Special Force and Regulars in Korea

F OR weeks after the invasion there was uncertainty as to what, if any, contribution Canada should make to the land forces of the United Nations opposing the North Koreans. In July, three destroyers and a transport squadron of the RCAF were placed under UN command. It was only on 7 August that the Prime Minister announced that a brigade group would be specially recruited for service in Korea, where it would operate as part of a Commonwealth Force. Second battalions would be raised for each of the regular infantry regiments. They were to be recruited from volunteers, preferably veterans, and would have special terms of service. It was not possible to send the existing regular units to Korea, for they were committed to operational roles under agreements with the United States.

Lest the voters imagine that the Canadian Government was agreeing to any permanent expansion of the Army, these volunteers for Korea would not be enlisted as regulars in the normal way, but would belong to a 'Special Force'. Their terms of service would be for eighteen months, or more if the emergency so required. In practice this came to mean that they had an obligation to serve in Korea for one year, providing they arrived there within the term of their engagement. Some thus served for eighteen months only, others for several months more. Inevitably this caused some discontent.

The Special Force was conceived in haste and it caused a host of administrative problems which took far too much of the time of over-worked units and staffs. The Government had not foreseen the course of world events and the commitments which Canada would have to undertake. Soon the Army would have forces in Germany as well as Korea and no one could forecast when they might be withdrawn. In less than two years, the Special Force soldiers would be disappearing from the muster rolls, their places taken by new regulars of the expanded forces. But in 1950 the volunteers did not concern themselves with such subjects. They came forward in droves.

For four months the raising of the 2nd Battalion became the full time occupation of the 1st. On 8 August Currie Barracks was flooded with recruits. The 1st Battalion enrolled, equipped, housed and trained them. They ran refresher courses for officers and NCOs. The commanding officer of the new battalion was to come from the Reserves, as, it was hoped, would most of his men. The Patricias were delighted when Lt-Col J. R. Stone, DSO, MC, who had commanded the Loyal Edmonton Regiment with such distinction in Italy was selected.

The help given by the 1st Battalion in raising the new unit was unstinted. It was soon apparent that the most pressing need of the 2nd Battalion was for trained NCOs. Col Cameron handed Col Stone the nominal roll of his sergeants and invited him, in consultation with his Regimental Sergeant Major, to select half of them.

In the early stages of the North Korean invasion things went badly for the South Koreans and the US Forces who came to their aid. For some time it seemed possible that the Communists would win an all-out victory, and no force from Canada could help prevent it. When the situation stabilized it was realized that at least a brigade group would be required. Later, after the brilliant landings at Inchon, with the North Korean forces being tumbled back to the Yalu River, it was decided to send only one Canadian battalion to Korea, the remaining units being held at a US Army Camp, Fort Lewis, near Seattle. The 2nd Patricias, now training at Camp Wainwright, were chosen.

They sailed from Seattle on 25 November in a United States Army Transport, the *Private Joe P. Martinez*.

In September, Lt-Col Cameron, the CO of the 1st Battalion had been promoted to command the Royal Canadian School of Infantry at Camp Borden. He was replaced by Lt-Col N. G. Wilson-Smith, MBE, a former Militia officer of the Royal Winnipeg Rifles.

The 1st were now training and holding in Calgary a pool of reinforcements for service in Korea. Another company of reinforcements was in Fort Lewis. When the 2nd Battalion sailed these were gathered together in a new battalion of the Regiment, the 3rd, under command of Lt-Col G. C. Corbould, DSO, ED, who had commanded the Westminster Regiment (Motor) in the Second World War. Thirteen officers and sixteen NCOs of the 1st Battalion were posted to it.

The intervention of the Chinese in North Korea brought yet another change in Canadian plans. It was now obvious that the whole of the 25th Canadian Infantry Brigade (as the force was now called) would be required and 3rd battalions were authorized for the other regular infantry regiments.

Upon the departure of the 2nd, the 1st Battalion began to put its house in order. Advanced airborne training and exercises took place. A camp was set up at Vernon in British Columbia to train Korean drafts and for refresher training for men of the battalion. It became routine for visitors to drop into the school by parachute. The battalion's NCOs School arrived by that route for battle training, along with the Commanding Officer and the Paymaster, with his money in a special pack. Later the battalion hockey players arrived that way, complete with their equipment to play the local Vernon team.

A large number of reinforcements were being held by the battalion, waiting for the 3rd to move from Fort Lewis to Camp Wainwright. In May it was announced that another Canadian brigade group would be raised for service in Europe. Many officers and men of the 1st Battalion were required to help with its training. Fewer than one-third of the officers and a slightly higher proportion of the NCOs were present with the unit although its strength with reinforcements was about 1,500. In July most returned, and some even had leave.

On 19 August, the Commanding Officer announced that the 1st Battalion would relieve the 2nd in Korea. A and C Companies would leave in one month's time. One parachute company with 150 additional jumpers with an 'appropriate rank structure' would remain to carry out the battalion's operational commitments, their places being taken by men from the 3rd.

There was much to be done. The effect of leaving so many trained men behind was most noticeable in the rifle companies. On 19 August, A Company was comprised of completely trained parachutists. When it sailed from Seattle on 21 September, it had only 28 of its original 137 members. It had had time for only one brief tactical exercise in Sarcee Camp in the month of September. Individually however, the officers, NCOs and men were well trained. It would not take long in Korea to make them a fighting team.

A and C Companies were followed two weeks later by Battalion Headquarters, HQ Company and D Company. The final flight of the Battalion – B Company and Support Company sailed from Seattle on 19 October.

During the winter of 1950–51, the 3rd Battalion was at Fort Lewis. By the new year, it had taken over 1st's responsibility of reinforcing the battalion in Korea. For more than a year this was to be their main task until their turn came to take the field.

In March, 1951, Col Corbould was posted to the Far East and was replaced by his second-in-command, Major H. F. Wood. With the departure of the 25th Brigade for Korea, the Canadians were to vacate Fort Lewis and on 7 May the Patricias left for Wainwright.

In spite of shortages of clothing and equipment, the battalion succeeded in training large numbers of reinforcements, first for the 2nd Battalion, then for the 1st. Because of the isolation of Camp Wainwright, and the lack of amenities there, the 3rd was sent to Eastern Canada for the winter. On 22 September they moved to Camp Borden, Ontario, for two months, then to Camp Ipperwash, some thirty miles from Sarnia, on the shores of Lake Huron.

Early in 1952 the battalion was fleshed out to its full establishment. In May they moved back to Camp Wainwright for more advanced field training. Equipment shortages had been overcome and it was a well-trained unit that left from Seatttle on 6 October to relieve the 1st Battalion in Korea.

The three battalions of the PPCLI sailed to Japan in United

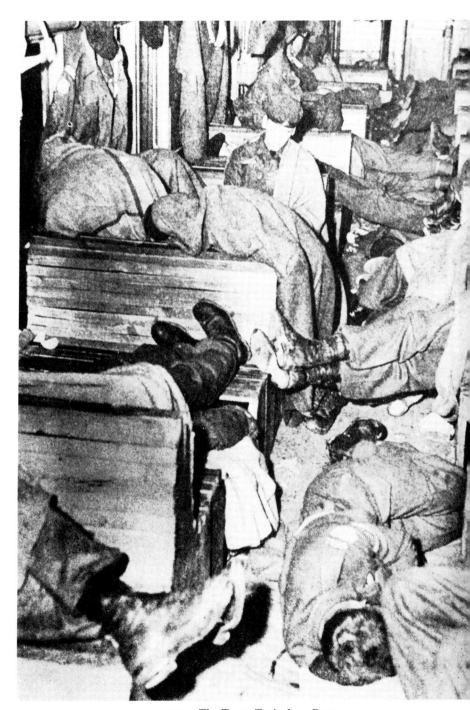

19. *The Troop Train from Pusan.*

20. *Officers of the 1st Battalion in Korea swear allegiance to HM Queen Elizabeth II on her accession to the throne, 10 February, 1952. Major J. C. Allan, Lts Frost and Davies, Lt-Col N. G. Wilson-Smith.*

21. *The Imjin Gardens, Winter, 1952.*

22. 27 *July*, 1953. *Capt C. A. H. Kemsley reads the cease-fire instructions to men of the 3rd Battalion.*

23. *Major E. J. Williams, A Company, 1st Battalion, at command post of Major E. J. H. Ryall, A Company, 2nd Battalion, reporting his return from raid on Hill 156. On left Lt-Col N. G. Wilson-Smith.*

24. *Lady Patricia Ramsay, accompanied by Lt-Cols J. R. Cameron and J. R. Stone, inspects a Guard of Honour commanded by Capt. R. K. Swinton, Calgary, 1953.*

States transports. From there some Patricias crossed Japan by rail, then took the short sea route from Sasebo to Pusan. Others continued by sea either to Pusan or Inchon, in US, British or Japanese ships. The 3rd Battalion went by train from Yokohama to Hiro, where they remained for a week's training before sailing on the British transport *Empire Pride* for Pusan.

In a unique way the story of the three Patricia battalions in Korea is a Regimental tale, for when one relieved another, they took over not merely their arms and their equipment, but their operational tasks and many of their men. From September, 1951, they never moved far from the same positions in the fighting line. The story covers the whole span of the Canadian participation in the Korean war, for the Patricias were the first to meet the enemy and they remained there until the shooting ended.

When the 2nd Battalion came to Korea, it was not at first apparent that the war differed so fundamentally from others in which the Regiment had been engaged. Canadians were not experienced in wars with limited aims, ones which could not be won. When the peace talks began in the summer of 1951 it became obvious that there was no question of a fight to the finish.

The battles in which the PPCLI took part in Korea were, on the whole, small affairs, seldom involving the whole battalion. The brilliant defensive battle of Kap'yong cost nothing like the number of casualties of Frezenberg or Sanctuary Wood. But in the daily routine of war men were often in as great danger as in other conflicts. Patrol actions could be vicious and expensive. Often shelling was as heavy as that met in the two world wars. But technically the UN forces were not at war. Restraints had been imposed on their operations in Korea; they were to fight – but not too hard. It was difficult within an infantry battalion to define the kind of restraint which was required. It was implicit that no operation should be undertaken which would be expensive in casualties. Certainly, every opportunity was taken to destroy as many of the enemy as possible, but in the minds of Canadian officers, the mere killing of Chinamen could never compensate for the loss of their own men.

Patriotism, or a sense of fighting to defend the homeland, could play little part in inspiring the troops. But being in a Commonwealth Force, serving among larger numbers of Americans and Koreans led to some interesting manifestations of pride. There was not a man in the PPCLI who did not firmly believe that the Patricias were the best soldiers in the Canadian Brigade. He admired and liked the men he met in the other units of the Commonwealth Division, and accepted that they were almost as good as the Canadians. There was no question in his mind but that the Commonwealth Division was far superior to any other Allied formation in Korea. He knew that even the Chinese appreciated this fact, since they were much more reluctant to attack his division than the others on the front. He knew, too, that any action fought by the Regiment was watched and discussed by the other units of the Brigade as well as by the British, Australians, New Zealanders and Indians of the Division. It mattered greatly to him what they thought of the Patricias. He did not often think of the enemy. He spoke of the Chinese as 'the laundrymen' and felt rather sorry for them.

The men of the three battalions had many experiences in common. They found little to attract them in Korea. The towns were poor, overcrowded and dirty, and they had little contact with the people. Much time was spent in patrolling and raiding. All battalions were attacked by the enemy and spent boring periods in reserve. Most men, too, spent five days in Tokyo on 'R and R' (rest and recuperation) leave, which gave them something to talk about during their remaining service in Korea.

Visitors to the officer's mess tent of the 1st Battalion sometimes asked why a steel helmet, a parachute helmet and a kimono hung from the tent pole. It was explained that they were a manifestation of the innate modesty of the Regiment. Officers were only permitted to tell their personal experiences of fighting, jumping, or R and R leave if they were prepared to put on the appropriate article of clothing.

As the 2nd Battalion sailed for Korea on 25 November, 1950, the war seemed to be nearing its end. Their most likely role would be in an army of occupation. While they had yet to do any serious advanced training, this could be completed if necessary in Korea. The Director of Military Training estimated that they would not be ready for action until 15 March, 1951.

On arriving in Yokohama on 14 December they learned that the picture had changed drastically. When Col Stone reported to 8th Army Headquarters in Korea, the Commanding General wanted to commit the untrained battalion at once, but Col Stone's instructions were explicit – 'In the event that operations are in progress when you arrive in Korea, you are not to engage in such operations, except in self-defence until you have completed the training of your command and are satisfied that your unit is fit for operations. This restriction in your employment has been communicated to the Commander United Nations Forces Korea'.

If the last sentence were correct, the commander of the 8th Army apparently had not seen it. Col Stone was well aware of the reasons for the restriction. The disaster which had befallen the partly-trained Canadian battalions in Hong Kong in 1941 was fresh in the minds of the Government and they would not allow him to deviate from his directive. When his verbal explanation was not accepted, he had no choice but to produce his instructions. At once the Army Commander agreed to the battalion proceeding with a further eight weeks of training. The episode had been most distasteful to Col Stone, particularly since many American units had been thrown into action with less training than the Patricias. Lt-Col H. F. Wood in *Strange Battleground* comments 'The consequences of sending troops out of Canada before they had completed their training had once again been demonstrated. No lives were lost because of it, but the embarrassment of having to turn down an operational commitment remained (to say nothing of the trouble caused) out of all proportion to the size of the contribution. It is perhaps fortunate that Eighth Army reaction has not been recorded.'

Meanwhile, on 18 December, the battalion landed at Pusan. There they remained for nine uncomfortable days, before moving

15 miles north to Miryang. They were glad to be out of the filth of the Korean port.

For a month the battalion trained in hill tactics, developed its operational procedures and learned to use the US mortars and machine guns with which it was now provided.

The fluctuations of the war had left many guerillas hiding in the hills near the battalion's training area. The 16th Field Regiment, Royal New Zealand Artillery had lost two men killed and two wounded in guerilla attacks and on 16 January a Patricia officer was wounded by a sniper's bullet. For several days companies of the PPCLI swept the surrounding area. Parties of guerillas were engaged and several were killed and wounded. The battalion regarded it as excellent training.

At the end of January Lt-Col Stone, after a final training exercise reported that they were ready for operations and on 9 February, the PPCLI moved to join the 1st Battalion, Middlesex Regiment, 1st Battalion Argyll and Sutherland Highlanders, 3rd Battalion Royal Australian Regiment, 16th Field Regiment, Royal New Zealand Artillery, and 60th Indian Field Ambulance in the 27th British Commonwealth Brigade.

In the two months of their offensive, which had begun on 26 November, the Chinese Communists had taken all of North Korea and had over-run almost a quarter of South Korea, including the capital city of Seoul. On 25 January, 1951, the UN counter offensive had begun. When the Patricias joined them, 27th Brigade was advancing up the centre of the peninsula south-east of Seoul. The enemy were withdrawing slowly, their rear-guards preventing contact with their main bodies.

The UN Forces depended upon the few roads of the country for the movement of their supporting arms and their supplies. Hence tactical objectives became the hill features from which movement on the roads could be controlled. In an advance the task of the infantry was to secure the successive dominating features which lay in their path. On 19 February the Patricias were given such a hill as their objective. There was no opposition, but the men received their first practical lesson of war. By the road they came upon the bodies of 65 American soldiers who had been surprised and killed while still in their sleeping bags. From that time Patricias used blankets in the front line in Korea.

It was three days later that the battalion made their first contact with the enemy. As the advance continued they had to drive the Chinese off the heights on both sides of the valley road. The hills were very steep and covered with low tangled bush. To climb them was difficult enough, but fighting their way up was a slow business indeed. For four days the Brigade's advance was blocked by strong forces which finally withdrew when the Australians' captured a dominating hill on the Patricia's flank. With their objectives secured, the Commonwealth troops waited until Allied formations caught up.

When the Brigade resumed their advance the grain of the country had changed. The valleys now ran from east to west across their path, the high ground above providing natural lines of defence for the enemy. 27th Brigade was to move across these to an objective eight miles to the north.

On 7 March the Patricias attacked the Chinese holding Hill 532. A Company, attempting to turn the left flank of the position made some progress, but the advance of D Company moving directly against the enemy was slowed by machine-gun fire. Air strikes and steady artillery and mortar fire failed to neutralize the enemy. The attack became a series of stubbornly-fought section battles. A Company, moving along a ridge line, were blocked by a succession of enemy posts. There was no room to manoeuvre and they were obliged to halt and dig in. About 2 pm D Company attacked again. They succeeded in getting some men on top of the objective, only to find they were under fire from a yet higher hill beyond. Col Stone instructed the company to withdraw, while moving B Company forward to hold the base of the enemy hill, closing the gap between the two forward companies. They spent a cold and uncomfortable night close to the enemy outposts. The veteran Chinese soldiers holding them spent the night hurling grenades down onto B Company. The sound of them laughing increased the Patricias' anger. By 5 am they had had enough. Quietly, they fixed bayonets, then charged up the hill. Most of the enemy had gone, but 47 Chinese dead lay on it when, by 9 am, B Company had secured the last objective.

D Company was not alone in failing to achieve success on the previous day, for the units on the flanks had fared no better. The company had fought well, and suffered 34 casualties. Typical of the aggressive spirit shown by the Patricias was the behaviour of Pte L. Barton, the leading platoon commander's batman. When his officer and several members of the platoon were wounded, he took charge and led the advance, though he himself was wounded three times. He continued until he was ordered to the rear. Much of the ultimate success of the battalion's attack was attributed to his bravery. He was awarded the Military Medal, the first Canadian to be decorated in the Korean war.

Surprisingly, the Chinese now broke contact. The Brigade advanced across the difficult country until 13 March when it was relieved by a regiment of the 1st US Cavalry Division.

Their three weeks in action had cost the 2nd PPCLI 57 casualties. They had learned that their training was sound and that their enemy was well trained and dangerous. The morale of the battalion was excellent.

On 17 March the Colonel-in-Chief's birthday was celebrated with a parade, a sports meet in the afternoon, a beer issue, and a concert by the Argyll's pipe band. Seoul had been liberated and the Chinese Communists were pulling back across the North Korean border.

The Patricias joined the advance on 29 March, when the 27th Brigade was given the task of advancing up the Chojong River, almost due east of Seoul in the middle of the peninsula. There were no roads on which a vehicle could move on the Patricia's axis of advance and the battalion was supplied by trains of Korean porters. The hills rose 1,500 to 2,000 feet above the valley floors and their crest lines were broken by gullies and steep rock faces. In places the snow lay four to five feet deep. There was no serious resistance and in two days the Brigade had advanced to the head of the Chojong valley. It now moved five miles to the east and was directed up the valley of the Kap'yong River. Its objective lay a few miles north of the 38th parallel in North Korea.

For the first few days the Patricias followed up other battalions of the Brigade. On 8 April they crossed the 38th parallel and again took up the lead on the Brigade's right flank. A few casualties were suffered in driving the enemy from the final objectives, which were reached on 16 April. On the 19th, the 27th Brigade was relieved by the 6th Republic of Korea Division and moved south into reserve, immediately north of the village of Kap'yong. The New Zealand Artillery remained in support of the South Korean troops.

Late in the evening of 22 April the Chinese struck in great strength against the Republic of Korea troops to the north. By the next morning, the front collapsed. Great anxiety was felt for the New Zealand gunners and the company of the 1st Middlesex who had remained with them to protect the guns. The Brigade Commander despatched the remaining three companies of the 1st Middlesex, by forced march, to help. To the rear, the Argyll and Sutherland Highlanders were being replaced by the 1st Kings Own Scottish Borderers. Thus when the Brigade was ordered to secure the escape route of the withdrawing Allied forces, only the 2nd PPCLI and the 3rd Royal Australian Regiment were available for the task.

Near the Brigade's bivouac area, the valley of the Kap'yong River narrowed and wound between two large hills. The Australians occupied one to the east of the river, the Patricias the one to the west. During the afternoon, the Middlesex and New Zealanders returned to the Brigade area.

The first Chinese attacks fell upon the Australians about 10 pm on 23 April. All night they continued and by next morning had penetrated as far as their battalion headquarters. The Brigade Commander knew that there was little hope that the Australians could hold out for another night and ordered them to withdraw. As the RAR fought their way to the rear, the Chinese turned their attention to the 2nd PPCLI.

The battalion was deployed to cover the north face of Hill 677. A Company was on the right, C in the centre and B forward on the left. D Company held the highest position on the hill behind B. Battalion Headquarters was in the rear of the right hand company. With the loss of the Australian positions on the right, that flank was no longer secure and Col Stone moved B Company from the forward spur which it held to a position east of his headquarters, overlooking the river. As they were digging in the enemy could be seen moving in the valley. Shortly after 10 pm the attack was launched and one section position was penetrated before it was repelled. There followed two more in battalion strength, which succeeded in over-running most of a platoon position. A fourth assault was broken up by mortar fire. Then a fifth was launched around the company's right flank, in the direction of Battalion Headquarters. The company was powerless to interfere and informed Battalion Headquarters that in a matter of minutes it would be over-run. Fortunately for the Patricias the mortar platoon was equipped with American armoured half-tracks each of which mounted a .50 calibre machine gun. As the Chinese force charged toward Battalion Headquarters, it was met by their concentrated fire and that of the 81 mm mortars firing at their shortest range. The assault was literally blown back down the ravine.

By 2 am every weapon in the battalion was firing on the enemy. It soon became apparent that the heavy attacks on B Company and Battalion Headquarters were only diversions, as D Company was assaulted from two sides. In ten minutes the Chinese over-ran much of the company's position. The Company Commander brought down the fire of the New Zealand guns on top of it, but it was only after two hours that the enemy's advance was stopped. All night the Chinese persisted in their attacks but, as daylight approached, they were broken off and D Company was able to re-establish its former position.

The battalion by now was cut off from the rest of the Brigade and was under heavy fire. But the enemy launched no more assaults. Reserves of ammunition and rations were running low, when at 4 am Col Stone asked for supplies to be dropped by parachute to the battalion. Four C119 aircraft took aboard rations and the required and dropped them on the battalion by 10 o'clock that morning. Later in the day, the road to the rear was opened.

On 26 April 2nd PPCLI was relieved by a battalion of the 1st US Cavalry Division and moved back to the south-west with the Commonwealth Brigade to secure an area behind which badly mauled Allied units could reform.

At the time of the battle the Patricias did not appreciate the significance of the action at Kap'yong, nor did they regard it as a 'desperate struggle'. Indeed their casualties were remarkably light, 33 in all. Viewed from Eighth Army Headquarters it was a different matter. Had the Commonwealth Brigade not stopped the Chinese, major Allied forces might have been cut off and Seoul might have fallen again. They were grateful and awarded the United States Distinguished Unit Citation to the 3rd Royal Australian Regiment and the 2nd Patricias. It was some months before the Canadian Government agreed to the acceptance of the award and authorized the battalion to follow the American practice of carrying a blue streamer with the name of the action on the pike of their regimental colour. It was almost five years after the action before they authorized the men of the battalion to wear the ribbon.

The Chinese had shot their bolt. For the first weeks of May, the Patricias spent their time in improving the defences of reserve positions and in some limited patrolling. On the 20th they began to move with the 28th Brigade (Headquarters 28th Brigade had replaced HQ 27th Brigade on 25 April) toward the north, seeking to make contact with the enemy. On 27 May, 2nd PPCLI was transferred from the 28th Brigade to the 25th Canadian Infantry Brigade at Sambi-ri on the Han River.

The Canadian Brigade had arrived in Korea on the 4th of May and had been committed to action on the 25th. When the Patricias came under their command, they were taking part in an operation under 1st US Corps from which they were not released until 3 June. Before the battalion could join them physically, the Patricias were again attached to the 28th Brigade to establish a patrol base across the Imjin River from which other units could probe into Chinese territory.

It was not until the 10th that the PPCLI joined their old friends whom they had last seen in Fort Lewis.

On 19 June, the Brigade moved to the Ch'orwon area some 20 miles north of the 38th parallel and to the east of the Imjin River, where they relieved an American and a Korean regiment. For a month the Patricias fortified their exposed and uncomfortable position and carried out deep patrols to locate the enemy. There were few contacts and the stay at Ch'orwon is chiefly remembered for the discomfort of operating in very rough country in temperatures hovering around 100°F. The patrols were large affairs, usually consisting of a company with tanks and engineers. Artillery was moved forward of the battalion's position to support it. The Brigade's War Diary noted 'the lack of equally vigorous patrolling by the flanking units has made unprotected flanks ten to twenty thousand yards long quite common-place. To cover these flanks the individual battalions have been forced to expend a considerable force drawn from their patrol strength to picket their flanks in order to prevent surprise and encirclement of their patrols . . . For the most part the weather has been very hot and the danger of heat exhaustion in the hills is great. The length of the patrols and the height of the hills climbed, an average of 450 metres, makes this patrolling more tiring than is normal, with the result that the troops quickly become exhausted and at least one day of rest is essential before going on another patrol.'

Enemy opposition to the patrolling increased. At first it was confined to mortaring, but towards the end of June, he became more aggressive. On 11 July B Company lost six men in an ambush. A week later the Patricias were relieved by a battalion of the Turkish Brigade.

It was during the tour at Ch'orwon, on 10 July, that ceasefire negotiations began between the opposing military commanders. The protracted wrangling that resulted went on for two years and provided a quality of unreality to the Korean campaign.

A cause of much satisfaction was the official formation of the 1st Commonwealth Division on 28 July. In it were joined the 25th Canadian Infantry Brigade, 28th British Commonwealth Brigade and 29th British Infantry Brigade. It gave the Canadians the assurance that in future operations at least one of their flanks would always be secure.

Until early in September the Division held the Kansas Line, behind the Imjin River, with 25th Brigade in reserve. A series of deep patrols were carried out to ensure that the enemy were not building up forces north of the river. On 22 August 2nd PPCLI with the Royal 22e Regiment crossed the Imjin and established a firm base some five miles beyond it. They then swept the area to a depth of another four miles before turning south to return across the Imjin. A few small enemy units were flushed, but there was no serious opposition.

On 10 September the Canadian Brigade crossed the Imjin again to occupy a new defensive line. By mid-afternoon the Patricias had secured their sector and were digging in. There had been no opposition. Three weeks later, the Commonwealth Division again moved forward as 1st Corps closed on the enemy's main defences. The objective was called the Jamestown Line and would be familiar to all Canadians who subsequently served in Korea.

For the Patricias the advance began during the morning of 4 October. In the afternoon the Chinese defending D Company's objective fought stubbornly. A vicious little hand-to-hand melée resulted, which lasted for nearly four hours. The small garrison was wiped out, 24 Chinese being killed or taken prisoner. Elsewhere there was little resistance and by noon on 5 October 2nd PPCLI were firm on the Jamestown Line.

The battalion now set about building its defences. On the night of 11 October enemy fighting patrols attacked the Patricia's wiring parties. Two nights later the forward companies were heavily shelled and mortared, but the enemy assaults which followed were beaten off.

That same night A and C Companies of 1st PPCLI moved into reserve positions behind the 2nd Battalion and at first light on the 14th relieved C and D Companies in the forward area. The 2nd now had two A Companies. To avoid confusion they dubbed their own 'Able White' and the newcomers 'Able Green'.

Chinese patrols continued to probe the Patricias' defences for the remainder of the month. The hills were covered with thick undergrowth and it was at first relatively simple for the enemy to penetrate between the widely separated companies and they had experts to do it in the form of specially trained patrol units. During their first evening in the line a grenade was thrown at the Company Commander and CSM of Able Green from some nearby trees. A train of Korean porters was ambushed in the rear, and one morning a company commander checking his defences discovered that three of the trip flares covering his front had been removed from the ground and left in a neat pile, with their lengths of piano wire neatly coiled beside them.

Two could play at this game. The Patricias began using well-placed ambush patrols to bushwhack the enemy.

From the time that A and C Companies, 1st PPCLI, landed at Pusan on the morning of 6 October, until they moved off to the front six days later, they followed a route that was to become familiar to many Patricias. As they waited to board their train at a nearby siding, they met their first Koreans. For the most part these were small boys, who joked with the troops in broken English and offered to polish their boots. American military police soon appeared and chased the boys away, threatening them with their night-sticks. The ruthless attitude of the MPs seemed far too harsh to the Patricias until some of them noticed that their fountain pens or wallets were missing. One later remarked that a Korean would take anything that wasn't nailed down and if it was he'd fetch a hammer.

For 24 hours they made their way northward in what must have been some of the worst and oldest rolling stock in the world. Some coaches had wooden seats, others nothing but three tier plank bunks, no washing facilities and the crudest of toilets. The train commander, an elderly captain of the US Army Quartermaster Corps, regaled the Patricia officers with stories of the hazards of life in Korea. When he told how trains were sometimes ambushed by guerilas, the senior Patricia officer quietly ordered his Sergeant Major to issue fifty rounds of ammunition to each of the men and post lookouts to watch both sides of the track. The US captain protested that it was contrary to orders for troops moving by train to be in possession of ammunition. He was told that it was contrary to the Patricias standing orders to be surprised by the enemy. A cool but correct relationship was continued for the balance of the journey.

At Tokchong they were met by the second-in-command of the 2nd Battalion with transport to carry them to B Echelon south of the Imjin River. For four days they trained on new weapons and radio sets and climbed the hills of the Kansas Line, while officers and NCOs visited the forward areas.

Since there had been no time for tactical training for the two companies since they began to prepare for service in Korea in Calgary some six weeks before, it was decided that their move to the front should take the form of a tactical approach march. On 12 October they moved off in blistering hot weather, to move along the crest lines of the hills beyond the Imjin toward their new positions 20 miles away. Next afternoon they practised an attack with tanks, using live ammunition, their objectives being the hills on which they would spend the night, before relieving the 2nd Battalion on the following morning. A Company's was an old Chinese position which had been taken a week before during the advance to the Jamestown Line. It was necessary to bury several very dead Chinamen before supper. That night was spent on the alert as the 2nd Battalion beat off a Chinese attack.

On 23 October, a month after leaving Calgary, Able Green carried out a raid on Hill 156, part of the Chinese main defences some two thousand yards in front of the 2nd Battalion's forward companies. The attack was supported by artillery and tanks firing at long range. The object was to test the strength of the enemy, destroy protective bunkers and to direct artillery fire onto Chinese positions behind the objective.

The newcomers had the impression that they were putting on a performance since the whole line of their advance could be watched from the hills of the Canadian Brigade. Artillery support was heavy and accurate as A Company's platoons took successive small features on the ridge line leading towards the objective. Heavy machine gun fire from the main Chinese position was neutralized by a concentration of direct tank fire. Scarcely had the last round exploded when the two leading platoons were on the objective with the bayonet.

For more than two hours they blew up Chinese defensive works and engaged targets to the rear while a company of 2nd PPCLI cleared a hamlet which had been bypassed in the attack. They were then ordered to return to the battalion position. The Chinese soon became aware of their withdrawal and put down artillery fire across the Company's path. More casualties were suffered on the way back than in the assault itself.

During the time that the 2nd Battalion was training in Calgary, they had heard many stories of parachuting and arctic exercises from men of the 1st. As Able Green returned through their lines, one of the Kap'yong veterans called to a Bren gunner 'Hey Slattery, how did you like a taste of real soldiering for a change?'

'Call that soldiering, sonny? You should have been on Sweetbriar!'

Battalion Headquarters, Headquarters Company and D Company of the 1st Battalion landed at the Yellow Sea port of Inchon on 27 October and within a week had taken over from their 2nd Battalion counterparts. On 4 November B and Support Companies of the 1st arrived in B Echelon, having followed A and C Companies' route from Pusan. On the 5th there was an official handover ceremony between the two battalions in the rear area. When Col Wilson-Smith returned to his command post, he found D Company under heavy attack.

During the afternoon the Patricias' three forward company positions had been subjected to steady mortaring and shelling. Toward 6 pm the firing increased as self-propelled guns were brought into action by the enemy. The heaviest weight of fire was falling on D Company. The first attack which developed at 6.15 was stopped by rifle and machine gun fire after suffering heavily from the defensive fire of guns and mortars. A second thrust about 8.15 was broken up by artillery. Half an hour later the Chinese moved to encircle the entire company. Wave after wave charged at D Company's wire with bangalore torpedoes, to be beaten off by small arms and grenades. About two hours after midnight, the enemy attacked again, some broke through the wire of two platoons and were finally stopped before they reached the Patricias' slit trenches. Gradually the action petered out.

It had been no mere raid. To quote the Unit War Diary 'The enemy had come prepared to stay. Each Chinaman was dressed in his khaki padded-cotton winter dress, and many had padded-cotton jackets rolled on their backs. Each had a shovel and carried cloth pouches of loose ammunition bandoliers and potato masher type hand grenades. Many rifles, burp guns, (SMGs) and two Russian-made Degtyarev LMGs were found near the dead.'

The character of the war had now changed in yet another way. When the 2nd Battalion had arrived there were fewer Chinese than North Koreans in the enemy's order of battle. By now the position was reversed. Not only were the Chinese better trained, they were supported by a far heavier weight of artillery and mortars. The concentrations which fell upon the positions held by the PPCLI and the King's Shropshire Light Infantry in the first days of November were as intense and accurate as any which those units had seen in the Second World War. The light field defences which had sufficed until now would have to be replaced by far more substantial works.

By the end of the war the defences of the Jamestown Line would have done credit to the Western Front in World War I.

Later in November the Chinese turned their attention to the units on the Patricias' immediate right. The battalion's machine guns and mortars were engaged in support of their friends but, apart from patrols, there was no direct contact with the enemy.

On 10 December D Company was in action again, this time in a raid to test the strength of new enemy positions on the battalion's right flank. Their objective was silhouetted against the clear night sky as the company moved off about 10 pm. The two leading platoons were close to the enemy when fire was opened, and they were greeted with a shower of grenades. For a time the raiders were held up, but the company commander, although wounded, lay in the open and passed back fire orders to supporting tanks. Soon the Chinese began to pull out and the third platoon, led by a corporal, assaulted through to the objective, whereupon the company was ordered to withdraw. They had suffered 25 casualties, including three of the four officers.

For the remainder of the winter contacts with the enemy were few. Christmas was celebrated over three days, companies in turn spending it at B Echelon where they were given a hot shower, clean clothes, turkey dinner, free beer, a movie and a night's sleep on a bed in a warm tent. On 18 January the battalion was withdrawn into reserve.

For six weeks the Patricias puttered about in a rear position. Training exercises and sports took up some of the time, but there was little to be done with spare hours in Korea. When the unit relieved the Welch Regiment on the Hook on 10 March the men looked upon it as an escape from boredom.

Patrolling and improving defences kept everyone fully occupied and the Chinese began to show more interest in the battalion's position by the west bank of the Sami-ch'on River.

During the night of 26 March an enemy force crept in to assault positions around No 7 Platoon of C Company which held an isolated hill. Within five minutes of the beginning of their artillery fire, the Chinese burst upon the Patricias, some succeeding in penetrating the wire behind platoon headquarters. They knocked out the covering machine gunner and for a few minutes it was touch and go. Sgt R. G. Buxton, in command of the platoon, though wounded, took over the gun and drove them back.

For several hours the attack continued. Reserves of ammunition were destroyed and a relief force battled their way through with more. The hard-fought action cost the platoon thirteen casualties. Twice as many dead were left behind by the Chinese. The CO of the 2nd RCR could see the Patricias' mortars in action and later reported that the tempo of their fire never wavered despite heavy shelling by the Chinese.

On 15 April the 1st PPCLI were relieved on the Hook by a

battalion of the 1st Regiment of US Marines, and moved to the familiar positions they had held from October to January. Two weeks later, Col Wilson-Smith became GSO 1 of the Commonwealth Division, being replaced as CO by Lt-Col J. R. Cameron.

The routine of patrolling and maintenance of defences was followed until, on 29 June, the battalion again moved into reserve. Fighting patrols in platoon strength had become costly affairs. In one on 20 June more than half of the 37 men involved were casualties.

Searching for other ways of hitting at the enemy, the Patricias looked to their 17 pounder anti-tank guns which had a range and muzzle velocity somewhat comparable to the famous German 88. With the technical help of artillery officers, they formed an ad hoc battery of six guns which fired at targets beyond the range of the Division's 25 pounders. In the view of Divisional artillery officers 'the infantillery' contributed little, and orders were received to stop this unauthorized form of warfare.

Shortly thereafter, there was another contretemps with the gunners' headquarters. The artillery authorities would not permit observers of the Air Observation Post flight to direct the fire of infantry mortars from their aircraft. The Patricias felt that someone should have a look at the rear of a Chinese hill where they were sure that there were targets which could only be reached by the high-angle fire of their weapons. The OC Support Company, 1st PPCLI, a qualified pilot, borrowed a liaison aircract and directed a shoot. Again, displeasure was expressed from above.

Administratively too, the Patricias used their initiative. B Echelon, south of the Imjin, was developed into a kind of hotel with well-stocked canteen, messes, sleeping tents and a set of showers which were the battalion's particular pride. The heart of them was a two-man see-saw type fire pump, an ancient boiler and a motley collection of pipe salvaged from the ruins of a Korean village. Shower heads were made from beer cans. So successful were they that several other units in the Division borrowed the services of the sleek, gold-toothed Korean who built and operated the showers, to construct sets for them.

From 30 June until 8 August the battalion was in reserve, then relieved the 1st Royal Norfolk Regiment on the extreme right of the Commonwealth Division. Patrol clashes were frequent in the valley between the Canadian and Chinese positions and the battalion area was frequently shelled. Enemy attacks were made both on the Americans on the battalion's right flank and on the Royal Canadian Regiment holding Hill 355 on the left. The PPCLI engaged them by fire but during this tour in the line only patrols made direct contact. When they did it could be exciting.

On the night of 15 October the Patricias sent a patrol under Sgt J. H. Richardson to pin-point some well-concealed enemy positions across the valley. They were successful and just as Sergeant Richardson had called for artillery fire on them an enemy platoon moved in. In the words of his report, 'I saw a man running toward me. I started to ask him what he was up to, when he shot me in the stomach . . . so I shot him in the face. All hell broke loose.' A confusing fire fight developed in which the Patricias lost eight more wounded and two killed. Sgt Richardson, wounded in five places, extricated his small force and called down artillery fire to hold off the enemy. The patrol withdrew, bringing their wounded with them, Richardson carrying Sgt Prentice of the snipers across his shoulders.

Next day the 1st Battalion was delighted to welcome Lt-Col H. F. Wood of the 3rd Battalion and five of his officers. On 26 October the battalion was relieved by a South Korean Regiment and moved back to a reserve position. There, on 3 November, the 3rd Battalion took over their responsibilities.

The 3rd had landed at Pusan, experiencing the now infamous ride to the North on the train which they described as 'sans lights, sans heat, sans beds, sans everything'. On 11 November the 1st said goodbye to their friends and embussed for the railhead. In the words of the War Diary, 'Farewells were said, songs were sung and universal two-fingered salute of the fortunate to the damned was given and returned in good natured derision.' As they boarded that train at Tokchong for Pusan, there was a moment of doubt as to who were the damned.

On the left of the Commonwealth Division, the 1st Black Watch had relieved the US Marines on the Hook. In the past few months, this important tactical feature had been the scene of heavy fighting as the Chinese launched powerful assaults to take it. Its loss could have meant the retirement of the Commonwealth Division from the Jamestown Line. The 3rd Patricias first task was to hold a company available to support the Black Watch should a counter-attack be necessary in their area. On 15 November the battalion rehearsed the plan as an exercise. Three days later it was necessary to carry it out as an operation of war, for in a violent attack the Chinese had succeeded in over-running some of the Highlanders forward positions. B Company, 3rd PPCLI, moved forward to replace the Black Watch reserve company, which was taking back the lost ground. The counter-attack was successful, but shortly after mid-night the Chinese gained another foothold on the Hook and a second company of the Patricias was moved forward. The fighting had ended by the time they arrived, but the Black Watch had suffered so heavily in the battle that the two companies remained under their command for several days and suffered their first casualties of the campaign.

On 1 December, the 3rd took over the Hook from the Black Watch. Though the battalion patrolled extensively there were few contacts with the enemy. It was, on the whole, a surprisingly peaceful tour. The troops were more bothered by the cold than they were by the Chinese.

On 28 December the Patricias were relieved by the Royal Canadian Regiment and spent two months in reserve. The regimental history notes that 'A tour in reserve involved so many in such boring duties that by mid-January many men were enquiring when they might expect another rest period in the front line. It was warmer in bunkers than in tents, and on the whole, the life was easier.'

At the end of January the entire Commonwealth Division was relieved by an American formation, and moved south of the Imjin. There followed a period of training exercises in which the skills of mobile warfare received a new polish. On 27 March Lt-Col Wood was evacuated sick, his place being taken by Lt-Col M. F. MacLachlan. On the 28th the battalion's strength was augmented by 100 Katcoms (Korean Augmentation Troops, Commonwealth Division). These were no 'rice burners', but combatant soldiers who were integrated into rifle sections and wore Patricia badges. At first there were problems of language, but the little men were soon taking a full part in the duties of the battalion.

On 6 April 3rd PPCLI returned to the line and relieved a Thailand battalion in the old positions which the 2nd Battalion had established on the Jamestown Line. Again it was a quiet tour, with only a few patrol clashes. It ended on the night of 13 May when the Patricias were relieved by 3rd Royal 22e Regiment.

They were again in the forward area early in June, having relieved 3rd RCR. Orders from Corps stated that patrolling was to be ·'restricted' but failed to define what that word meant. As a result the Patricias were out almost every night looking for the enemy. By now the Chinese were not patrolling vigorously, and though there were some fire fights and casualties to both sides, the tour was chiefly remembered for the heavy rains which caused a number of bunkers to collapse. On 9 July the battalion was relieved by the 1st King's Own Royal Regiment so that they might in turn relieve the 1st Royal Fusiliers on Hill 355 which had been the scene of so much heavy fighting. The war had now reached a standstill and although there was some harrassing mortar fire by both sides, little else occurred. The regimental history notes that 'The last hostile contact with the enemy is recorded in an intriguing item in the War Diary for 19 July "An enemy patrol is suspected of throwing stones at one of our patrols." '.

On 27 July the ceasefire became official. There was a great deal to be done in the next 72 hours for all defences were to be dismantled and stores withdrawn from the demilitarized zone. The Canadian reaction was unenthusiastic, not so the Chinese. At first light next day, the hills opposite the Canadian positions were 'crawling with men'. As an officer of 3rd PPCLI recalls, 'In the valley immediately below us, the Chinese had set up a platform with loudspeakers and banners announcing the "Peace". On the platform men and women were dancing and singing, but what impressed the troops was what looked like millions of Chinese opposing them. No one will ever forget the psychological impact of seeing for the first time the human sea.'

For three days the Patricias laboured under a sweltering sun to remove the enormous quantities of material from the hill positions. Early in August, they moved back to a permanent campsite, three miles south of the demilitarized zone. September was spent in constructing a semi-permanent camp and in preparing for the return of the 3rd Battalion to Canada. On 12 October the advance party of the 2nd Battalion Royal Highland Regiment of Canada (Black Watch) arrived and on the 29th the battalion moved by road to Inchon where they boarded the ship from which the Black Watch had just debarked.

Their days as a battalion were numbered. A new regiment, the Canadian Guards, was being formed, and non-parachutists of the 3rd Patricias were to be transferred to the 2nd Battalion of the new unit. Later this arbitrary dictum was modified and officers and men were given the alternative of remaining with the 1st or 2nd PPCLI. On 8 January, 1954, the 3rd was disbanded. It would be sixteen years before it was to reappear as a regular battalion of the Canadian Armed Forces.

Chapter 9
The Peacekeepers

WHEN 2nd PPCLI sailed from Seattle in 1950, it marked the last time that all units of the Canadian Army were in North America. The North Atlantic Treaty Organization had been formed to block further encroachments by the Soviet Union into Europe and plans were well advanced to despatch Canadian troops and aircraft to that continent. The United Nations were trying to keep other potential conflicts from developing and Canadian officers and men were seconded to the Organization for service in Asia, Africa and the Middle East. Life in the Regiment in peacetime was no longer routine or predictable.

On their return from Korea to Currie Barracks at Calgary, the 2nd became a parachute battalion committed to the defence of Canada. Then in 1953 they were warned for service in Germany. That summer, for the first time, the Regiment would be taking its families abroad.

The Patricias' new barracks in Germany was named Fort Macleod after the base of the North West Mounted Police in southern Alberta. It was near the village of Deilinghofen. The married quarters were in nearby Hemer on the eastern outskirts of the Ruhr.

The Regiment adjusted to living among their former enemies surprisingly easily. Until the Korean War they had fought scarcely anyone but Germans and at first it took a conscious effort to change the attitudes and habits of years. Officers and NCOs were reminded that they must no longer refer to the other side in a tactical exercise as the 'Krauts'.

One newly arrived major was taken to visit Sennelager, the former training area of the Kaiser's and Hitler's armies which was now used by NATO forces. The large black Iron Crosses carved in the stone entrance were a striking reminder of six years of war. He was looking back at them when his jeep stopped. He turned around to see a three-tonner in front disgorging German infantry – jack-boots, camouflaged jackets, MG 42s, Schmeisers, the lot. It was a startling experience.

From 1953 to 1957, the 2nd Battalion followed by the 1st served as foot-borne infantry in Germany. The battalion at home trained for the defence of Canada by parachute exercises in the North, and performed the host of ceremonial and administrative tasks that have always been the lot of armies with too many headquarters and too few units.

Almost the last ceremonial occasion of the 1st Battalion's tour in Germany was the planting of a maple tree which was to be the centre of the memorial to the Originals at Frezenberg, near Ypres. Four of them were there – Brig Gault, of course, and Lt-Cols Niven and Pearson and Sgt H. F. O'Connor. They found it difficult to recognize the battlefield of 1915 in the green, softly undulating Bellerwaerde and Frezenberg ridges. It was easier for them to sense the link between the immaculate guard of honour from the Regiment and the filthy haggard Patricias who had fought there forty-two years before.

In January, 1956, the Regimental Depot moved from Calgary to Edmonton where a new barracks was under construction. In the summer of the next year, they were joined there by the 2nd Battalion. To the delight of the Regiment, their new home was named the Hamilton Gault Barracks.

It was to Work Point Barracks at Esquimalt that the 1st Battalion returned in 1957. Few were left in the Regiment who had last served there in 1939 but the town and nearby Victoria welcomed the Regiment as their own. Both battalions were to remain in Canada until 1963 but the Regimental Band was not. As the 1st left Germany, they arrived to serve for two years with the 4th Canadian Infantry Brigade Group.

The variety of operational tasks for which the battalions now trained was bewildering. For three years, the threat of a nuclear attack on North America loomed so large in the minds of the Government that the Army was given the role of co-ordinating civil defence or 'National Survival' operations. The Patricias

learned the techniques of rescue and fire fighting, nuclear deconta-
mination and crowd control. Airborne operations in the Arctic and
amphibious landings on the West Coast were also rehearsed. They
prepared to fight in Europe as motorized infantry in the most
sophisticated of possible military environments and to operate
with a United Nations force anywhere in the world.

Officers and NCOs of the Regiment served in Indo China,
Ghana, Tanzania, the Middle East, Kashmir, the Congo and
Cyprus. In May, 1958, Lt-Col George Flint, seconded to the United
Nations Truce Supervisory Organization was killed by a sniper
while arranging for the evacuation of wounded men on Mount
Scopus near Jerusalem.

In December 1961, Capt Roger Beauregard won the MBE for
his gallantry in operating an isolated and essential signals station
in the Congo in the face of attacks and shelling by Katangan forces.

Training in Canada was not without its hazards. In 1959, S/Sgt
B. W. Holligan of the 2nd Battalion was awarded the George
Medal for saving the life of a soldier who was being towed helplessly
behind an aircraft, his parachute fouled.

When, in the midst of the Korean War, Canada found it
necessary to send a brigade group to Europe, units of the Militia
had provided companies to form the first composite infantry
battalions of that force. This had not been a happy solution.
Nonetheless it might well be necessary to call on the Militia again
to expand the Regular Army in situations short of war. It was
decided to affiliate some of the more efficient units with regular
regiments to facilitate the plan. The PPCLI were delighted when
the Loyal Edmonton Regiment was linked with them. In both the
First and Second World Wars, this fine regiment had been brigaded
with the Patricias and had come to typify the fighting qualities of
the Western Canadian Infantry in the eyes of the Army.

On 28 November, 1958, Brig Andrew Hamilton Gault died in
Montreal.

As the Founder, with Cols Farquhar and Buller, he had moulded
the Regiment to its original shape. Surviving them, he continued
to influence its style and spirit as no other could. If the Patricias

have a panache, a light-hearted competence, a sense of dedication, the roots are in him. He was a superb leader and an idealist. He made men believe in the military virtues of duty and honour and the traditions of the Regiment. He gave them confidence in themselves and a standard to emulate.

Young officers were in awe of the stern figure in the official portraits and photographs. But when they met with his charm and gaiety of spirit they worshipped him.

Away from the Regiment, he was no ordinary man. Despite his one leg, he was a superb horseman and in England won a reputation for daring in the hunting field. In the twenties, he learned to fly and with his wife who followed his example, piloted their small biplane to places as far away as Egypt and the Balkans. He was successful in business and finance, held a seat in the British Parliament, and was a generous and unpublicized philanthropist. His modesty was the despair of the Regiment's official historians. He adamantly expunged from their drafts such references to himself as Farquhar's disappointment when his recommendation of Gault for a VC brought instead a DSO, his generosity to the Regiment and his help to former soldiers in the Depression.

His appointment as Colonel of the Regiment passed to the senior serving Patricia, Brig Cameron Ware, DSO, CD.

In 1958, the exchange of officers with the allied regiment of the British Army, the Rifle Brigade, was re-instituted. Adventure training became popular and in addition to the normal training exercises in the Arctic, several expeditions were mounted by the Regiment. Two in 1963 and 1964 were to explore the inaccessible Nahanni River in the Northwest Territories. In 1965, another traversed the overland route taken in the gold rush to the Klondike in '98. Two years later, as part of the Canadian Centennial Celebrations, men of the Regiment attempted to find relics of Sir John Franklin's expedition in the islands of the Arctic archipelago.

In 1963, the 1st Battalion relieved the Queen's Own Rifles at Fort Macleod in Germany and were followed three years later by the 2nd. The battalions were now mechanized, rifle platoons being equipped with armoured personnel carriers. Versatility was as always the watchword and the need for it was often demonstrated. In one major training exercise, a company was required to move several miles to rendezvous with a group of Wessex helicopters of the Royal Air Force, leave their carriers, reorganize as an airborne assault force and carry out a helicopter landing behind an enemy-held river line – all in four hours of first being warned for the task.

To mark the 50th anniversary of the founding of the Regiment, the Colonel-in-Chief proclaimed 1964 to be its Jubilee Year. The 1st Battalion in Germany and the 2nd in Edmonton, as well as members of the Regimental Association in Canada and Britain celebrated with enthusiasm. The focus of the Regimental ceremonies were the presentations by Lady Patricia Ramsay, the Colonel-in-Chief, of wreaths of laurel to be worn on the Regimental Colours of both battalions. First at Fort Macleod in Germany, then in the Hamilton Gault Barracks, Edmonton, the Battalions trooped their Colour and Lady Patricia repeated the ceremony she had first performed at Bramshott in England, in 1919.

Earlier in the year the Regiment was awarded the Freedom of Ypres, the first time in history that such an honour had been bestowed by the Belgian city.

Veterans of the Regiment with the Regimental Band and the Drums of the 2nd Battalion were inspected on Parliament Hill in Ottawa, by the Prime Minister. In Europe, detachments attended the Liberation ceremonies at Calais, and the Remembrance Day parade at Vimy Ridge. In Canada a detachment of the 2nd Battalion represented the Canadian Army at Bisley, and won the Mappin Trophy, the Falling Plates Match as well as placing highly in other competitions. In Germany the Patricia team was placed second in the Prix Leclerc, the NATO small arms competition. Pte C. Petit won the British Army Heavyweight Boxing Championship, while Ptes M. R. Grey Eyes, R. A. Harrington, and Cpl H. W. Reti were Canadian Army boxing Champions in their weights. This year also the 1st Battalion was presented with the Hamilton Gault Trophy, the Army marksmanship prize which they had won in 1963.

Yet with all this, normal work still went ahead and Patricias took part in training exercises as far apart as the Western Arctic and Lünenberg Heath.

On returning to Canada in 1966, the 1st Battalion moved to the Home Station at Edmonton. Two years later they served for six months as part of the United Nations force in Cyprus. Theirs was the Kyrenia Sector, an area extending from the capital of Nicosia to the north coast and including the major Turkish enclave of that troubled island – some 550 square miles. Within it were the greatest concentrations of factional Cypriot troops as well as mainland Greek and Turkish regular units located on Cyprus by treaty. The Patricias task was, in part, to 'prevent a recurrence of fighting'. It involved constant vigilance from observation posts, and patrols and rapid intervention to stop a minor incident from escalating. It was the Regiment's first experience of such an operation and they learned much from it.

While the 1st were in Cyprus, the Home Station of the Regiment was moved to Currie Barracks in Calgary and it was to there that the Battalion returned.

The 1960s were a time of change in Canadian military policy. The Navy, Army and Air Force were integrated into a single unified organization, the Canadian Armed Forces. New uniforms and rank badges were adopted but the infantry regimental system continued. In the reorganization, the regular infantry was concentrated in the three old Permanent Force regiments, the Royal Canadian Regiment, the PPCLI and the Royal 22e Regiment plus the Canadian Airborne Regiment. In the process, a battalion of the Queen's Own Rifles of Canada became the 3rd Battalion Princess Patricia's Canadian Light Infantry.

In 1970 the 2nd Battalion returned to Canada. For twenty years, with only a few breaks, the Regiment had served as part of 1st British Corps in Northern Army Group. They would not return to Western Europe until 1984.

Coincident with their departure, the 4th Brigade Group moved to southern Germany to be located with the Canadian air squadrons of 2nd Allied Tactical Air Force. The Brigade now became part of Central Army Group. Lt-Col C. B. Snider and 198 other members of the 2nd Battalion formed the nucleus of one of its new units, 3rd Mechanized Commando of the Canadian Airborne Regiment, and were stationed at Baden Soelligen.

The employment of Patricia battalions as parachute units now came to an end. Officers and men of the Airborne Regiment were to come from other units to which they eventually would return. One of its components, 2nd Airborne Commando, came to be composed entirely of Patricias and a close link was formed between it and the Regiment.

With the formation of the 3rd Battalion in 1970, The Loyal Edmonton Regiment changed their supplementary title to 4 PPCLI.

As these organizational changes in the Canadian Forces were taking place, a new form of conflict began to concern the soldier – terrorism and civil disorder. In October, 1970, the War Measures Act was invoked in response to the actions of extremists in Quebec and the 1st and 2nd Battalions began intensive internal security training. Two companies of the 2nd were employed in the Montreal area during November searching for the terrorists whose movement collapsed at the end of that month as a result of the firm stand taken against them.

When in March, 1971, the 1st Battalion relieved the 3rd in Cyprus and the 2nd followed them in October of the next year, few realized that the pattern which they established would continue for years to come. The Canadian Contingent had moved from the hills above Kyrenia to the capital, Nicosia, and men of the Regiment were stationed on the Green Line, so named from the colour of a pencilled line drawn by an officer on a map when the Allied Regiment, the Rifle Brigade, first separated Greek and Turk along it in 1963.

Greek and Turkish posts in some places were only ten yards apart, often manned by tense and poorly trained boys. Any minor incident was dangerous, for both sides were prone to react emotionally and violently to any infringement of the local rules. The Patricias manning observation posts between them watched for any sign of trouble so they could quell it before it developed.

There were incidents every day demanding tact and firmness. Fortunately not many were so dramatic as one when a seventeen-year-old Turk loaded his sub-machine gun and accidentally loosed off twenty rounds into the air. The nineteen-year-old Patricia private in the nearest UN post ran to the scene and wrenched the weapon from the boy's hands. He raced across to the Greek post where another youth was nervously fingering the trigger of a machine gun and explained that the firing had been a mistake. Then he returned to the Turkish post to give the NCO in charge a dressing-down for training his men so badly.

Another PPCLI private revived a Greek sentry who had collapsed and apparently died of heat prostration. One of the observation posts spotted smoke coming from a roof and had the Fire Brigade on the scene before the occupants knew their house was on fire.

In all these peacetime tasks, the Regiment operated with the relaxed competence which marks the professional. They knew that their value as peacekeepers lay ultimately in their ability to fight. The Soviet officers who saw their intensive training exercises in Germany, and the Greeks and Turks who observed their battle efficiency tests in Cyprus, were keenly interested in knowing if the good-humoured young Canadian soldiers still kept their fighting skill.

When the 2nd Battalion arrived in Winnipeg from Germany, it marked the permanent return of the Regiment to that city after an absence of twenty-six years. The occasion was celebrated officially by a parade in Assiniboine Park in June, 1972, and by the granting of the Freedom of the City of Winnipeg to the Patricias.

In that year the Regiment mourned the passing of two who had not served in its ranks yet had secured a firm place in its affections. In September, Dorothy Gault, the widow of the Founder, died at their home in England. Ten days later, the death of Admiral Sir Alexander Ramsay, husband of the Colonel-in-Chief, ended the fifty-three years of his association with the Regiment.

Mrs Gault, 'DB' to her friends, was a frequent visitor to the battalions in Germany and Canada, sometimes to present the Hamilton Gault Trophy or to attend other regimental occasions. A remarkable leader in her own right, her beauty was matched by her courage. She rode well and was one of Britain's first women pilots when flying was an adventure. Her home at Hatch Court in Somerset was always open to visiting Patricias. Since her death, a small museum has been opened in the house which contains memorabilia of Hamilton Gault's military and political careers and of his and his wife's love of flying.

A little more than a year later, on 12 January, 1974, Lady Patricia Ramsay died in Surrey, almost sixty years from the time the Regiment was formed. She often remarked that the happiest days of her life were those spent in Ottawa before the outbreak of the First World War. Her father, the Duke of Connaught, had chosen a congenial and highly competent staff to serve him as Governor-General and they and their wives became Princess Patricia's closest friends. Alexander Ramsay whom she married was the naval ADC. Many young Canadians were welcomed to the circle, one of whom was Hamilton Gault.

When the Regiment was formed by Gault and Francis Farquhar, Captains Buller and Newton from Government House and others of her circle joined. She was immensely proud of her Regiment's achievements but its record was marked by the death or crippling injury of her close friends. Not surprisingly in later years, she looked upon it as a living memorial to the men who had set such high standards for it to follow. She fostered its well-being with affection and pride. For its part, the Regiment adored her.

Her father had been Colonel-in-Chief of The Rifle Brigade for over fifty years and it pleased her to think that together they were in the unique position of having more than 100 years' service as Colonels-in-Chief of the two Allied Regiments.

Characteristically she wanted only a simple funeral. It was held privately at St George's Chapel in Windsor Castle attended by her family, the Queen, members of the Royal Family, the Queen of Denmark and other foreign relatives. At her request, the Colonel of the Regiment, Maj-Gen C. B. Ware, a bearer party and two buglers alone represented the thousands who had worn her name.

As early as 1966, she had made it known that, subject to the wishes of the Regiment, she would prefer her successor as Colonel-in-Chief to be her god-daughter, Lady Brabourne, a cousin named after her and a great grand-daughter of Queen Victoria. The Regiment was delighted, the Queen approved and the new Colonel-in-Chief accompanied by her distinguished father, Admiral of the Fleet Lord Mountbatten of Burma, visited the battalions in Canada. In Calgary she took the salute when the 1st Battalion Trooped the Colour on 10 August, the sixtieth anniversary of the signing of the Regiment's charter.

Whilst not strictly correct to do so, it seemed only natural when the Regiment began to refer to her as 'Lady Patricia'.

The Sixtieth Jubilee was celebrated as enthusiastically as the Fiftieth. In Victoria, the Freedom of the City was accepted on behalf of the Regiment by the 3rd Battalion who later Trooped the Colour. In Winnipeg, the 2nd Battalion's arrangements were interrupted when they were called out for flood control operations on the Red River. Later they sent a small expedition to the Northwest Territories to climb Mount Hamilton Gault. A detachment marched from Port Arthur to Winnipeg following the route taken by Colonel Garnet Wolseley's force to Lower Fort Garry in 1870, their Pioneers assisted in the reconstruction of St Peter's, an historic church which dates from 1836, and another detachment undertook a canoe trip of 635 miles from The Pas in Manitoba to Lower Fort Garry and re-enacted the arrival of the Red River settlers. On 6 October, a memorial stone was unveiled at Lansdowne Park·in Ottawa, the Regiment's birthplace.

1974 was also the Jubilee of the Royal 22ᵉ Regiment. To mark their friendship, the regiments exchanged platoons, one from the Patricias spending a week in Quebec City during the Winter Carnival, whilst a similar number of 'Van Doos' came to Calgary for the 'Stampede'.

In November, 1975, twenty-five years after the arrival of the Regiment in Korea, a memorial was unveiled on the banks of the Kap'yong River within view of the 2nd Battalion's old positions. At the same time, the Regiment established an annual bursary to provide for the secondary education of a child of the district. The first of these awards was made in 1976 and the practice has continued since.

Earlier that year, a composite company of the Patricias and the

Canadian Airborne Regiment trained in Australia with the 6th Battalion of the Royal Australian Regiment whilst a company of that Regiment's 1st Battalion served with 1 PPCLI. Subsequently further exchanges took place, the Canadians learning about jungle warfare whilst the Australians exercised in the Arctic and in mountain and river operations in the Rockies.

To cement the friendship between the two regiments, which was born when they fought beside each other in Korea, the Queen approved their mutual wish to become Allied Regiments on 6 September, 1977.

'Training exchanges' by platoons or companies were a new development which continued from the middle of the 1970s. Sub-units of the Regiment have been attached to the Norwegian and German armies and have travelled to many major bases in the United States to train with the US Army and Marine Corps. Close to home, the British Army Training Unit at Suffield, Alberta, has included Patricia company groups in many of their valuable live-firing exercises. In the summer of 1979, 3 PPCLI and a company group of the 1st took part in the largest US/Canadian Amphibious exercise since the Second World War, embarking at San Diego and landing on the north of Vancouver Island. Three years later, a detachment of the 3rd landed in the Aleutians as part of a US Marine Amphibious Unit.

Valuable and interesting though such training proved to be there is always an aspect of unreality about the best of exercises. A new sense of purpose becomes evident when units are given a real job of work to do. Operations 'in aid of the civil power', even of the most unmilitary kind, have a unique training value of their own. Several times in the past, the Regiment had fought floods and forest fires. Their experience was repeated when the Red River burst it banks in 1974 and 1978 and when disastrous forest fires broke out north of Prince Albert, Saskatchewan, in 1977. In 1975 the 2nd and 3rd Battalions were obliged to take over the guarding of several Federal penitentiaries when their staffs went on strike. During the period whilst they were in control none of the inmates chose to challenge the authority of the soldiers. In 1976 the 1st Battalion and a detachment of the 3rd Battalion provided for security at the Olympic Games in

Chief.

carried by the Regiment in all their actions of the First World War. Known affectionately as the Ric-a-dam-doo, it was consecrated as the Regimental Colour in 1919.

27. *3rd Battalion landing on Amchitka in the Aleutian Islands, 1983.*

28. *'TOW' anti-tank missile firing at Suffield, Alberta.*

29. *PPCLI Battle School, Colonel-in-Chief autographing platoon pennant.*

30. *Parade to mark the 50th Anniversary of the Battle of Frezenberg at the Menin Gate, Ypres, May, 1965.*

31. *Cycle Patrol along the Green Line, Cyprus, 1971.*

Montreal. Two years later in 1978 the Pioneer Platoon of the 1st took part in the search for the fallen Soviet Cosmos 954 nuclear powered satellite in the Northwest Territories. Their task in bitter January cold was to assist in the construction of a 5,000 foot airstrip and base camp, a far cry from the traditional duties of infantry pioneers.

Adventure training also continued. One of the larger expeditions took place in August, 1978, when 100 men of the 3rd Battalion accompanied by eight soldiers from the 39th US Infantry Regiment completed the 600 mile trek from Skagway, Alaska, to Dawson City, Yukon, following the trail of the gold rush of 1898. The Company climbed the infamous White Pass, then travelled down the Yukon River in assault boats.

On 27 August, 1979, tragedy in its most violent form struck the family of the Colonel-in-Chief. During a holiday at Sligo Castle in Ireland, her father, Lord Mountbatten, her son Nicholas, her mother-in-law, the Dowager Lady Brabourne, and a local boy, Paul Maxwell, were murdered when a remotely controlled terrorist bomb was detonated in their boat. She herself and her husband Lord Brabourne and Nicholas's twin brother, Timothy, were severely injured. The Regiment's sense of outrage was only less than their concern and sympathy for Lady Patricia.

Lord Mountbatten had accompanied the Colonel-in-Chief on three visits to the Regiment and had fitted easily into the regimental family. In recognition he was made an Honorary Patricia. By his express wish, a thirty man guard represented the Regiment at his State Funeral in London.

It was with great relief and admiration that the Regiment welcomed the Colonel-in-Chief back to duty, first at the Frezenberg dinner of the United Kingdom Branch of the Regimental Association on 8 May, 1980, then in July when she visited the 3rd Battalion in Cyprus.

At an early stage of the unification of the Canadian Forces, the Regimental Depot was threatened with extinction. Such units were unheard of in the Navy and Air Force and it seemed logical to those inexperienced in the ways of infantry regiments that all recruits should be prepared for service in their battalions at one central location. After semantic battles more worthy of the law than the profession of arms, the Depot, officially disbanded in 1968, became the '1st Canadian Brigade Operational Training Detachment'. In 1981 it was renamed 'Princess Patricia's Canadian Light Infantry Battle School', a lieutenant-colonel's command, and moved to Camp Wainwright, Alberta. All young soldiers now received their initial training at the Canadian Forces Recruit School at Cornwallis, Nova Scotia. Before joining their battalions, new Patricias learned infantry techniques at the Battle School which also provided courses in special subjects such as winter warfare and helicopter operations.

Equipment continued to change. Battalions in the two world wars and Korea were infantry of the traditional kind in that they moved on their feet but in the 1960s their rifle companies became mounted, first in three-quarter ton trucks then in Armoured Personnel Carriers. Eventually the 2nd Battalion was equipped with the M113 whose tracked swimming capability did much for mobility. The 1st and 3rd Battalions received the Grizzly, a wheeled APC. Their advent brought a dramatic increase in firepower as each mounted both medium and heavy machine guns. Radios now were provided for each section and detachment and wire-guided anti-tank missiles, radars and night-fighting aids became standard equipment.

In the 1950s the faithful .303 Lee-Enfield rifle, two versions of which the Regiment had used since 1914, was replaced by the 7.62 mm FNC1, whilst the Bren was supplanted by the automatic FNC2. In 1984, a new rifle, the Colt C7, fully automatic and firing much lighter ammunition of 5.5 mm calibre replaced both the FN and the Sterling submachine gun and, to the relief of practising light machine gunners, the very effective 5.56 mm belt or magazine-fed MINIMI replaced the FNC2. For heavier support, units acquired the German belt-fed 7.62 MAG machine gun.

Beginning in the 1960s, battalions became increasingly involved in the use of helicopters. Hueys and Chinooks were used in air-landing and extraction operations and as platforms from which to parachute or rappel. For the many Patricias serving with the Airborne Regiment, even parachuting became more comfortable with the replacement of the T–7 with its teeth-rattling opening load by the more forgiving T–10, whilst others enjoyed free-falling with steerable para wings.

In 1983, the 4th Battalion were given the task of recruiting and training a parachute detachment to support the regular airborne forces, an indication of the high standard which they had achieved as militia.

Whilst none of the battalions had been stationed in Europe since 1970, much of their training was oriented towards NATO operations on that continent. In 1976 the 1st Battalion took part in a major exercise of the Allied Command Europe Mobile Force in Norway. Exercises in the high Arctic had as a background the preservation of Canadian sovereignty in the northern wilderness. The need to protect the chain of islands off Canada's West Coast lay behind the Regiment's amphibious training with the Navy and the US Marine Corps. From 1968 to 1984 there were only four years in which a Patricia battalion was not in Cyprus.

Apart from the men of the University Companies of the First World War, the private soldiers of the Patricias in the 1980s were the best educated men the Regiment had ever had. They were articulate, keen and quick to learn. The versatility which the Battalions had shown gave confidence that they would continue to operate as effectively in future as the Regiment always had.

But skill in the military arts is not enough. The infantry soldier is unique among those who fight in that he must advance into danger alone. Something makes him go on when his every instinct tells him to stop and take cover. (And that alternative is open to him as it is to no member of the crew of a ship or aircraft or even of a tank). Yet the infantryman is no braver, no more patriotic than other servicemen.

In the upheaval brought about by unification, the Canadian Forces recognized that the key to the infantryman's fighting spirit lay in the regimental system and they left it unchanged. No better example than the Patricias could be used to demonstrate its strength. At several stages, quite different sorts of men have made up the PPCLI – the old British Regulars of the Originals, the University men, conscripts, volunteers, the PF and the Canadian

Regulars and new Canadians of every racial background. All have
been imbued with the traditions of the Patricias and have gained
from them a sense of belonging to a unique fraternity. Particularly
in war, they felt strangely alone when away from their battalion,
at home when they returned. They knew they mattered to the
Regiment and the Regiment mattered to them. They developed
a near-proprietary interest in it. No matter what the Regiment
was called upon to do, they would do. They knew that if they held
back when it advanced into danger, they could never feel part of
it again.

Appendix I

OUTLINE OF SERVICE

1914–1984

1914 August	Regiment privately raised by Andrew Hamilton Gault in Ottawa for service with British Expeditionary Force. Named for Princess Patricia of Connaught.
October	Arrived Salisbury Plain – formed 80th Brigade with 3rd and 4th King's Royal Rifle Corps, 2nd King's Shropshire Light Infantry and 4th Rifle Brigade.
December	Only Canadian regiment in theatre of war in 1914.
1915	Ypres, Frezenberg, Bellewaerde.
December	Transferred to Canadian Corps. Joined Royal Canadian Regiment, 42nd Battalion (Black Watch) and 49th Battalion (Edmonton) to form 7th Brigade.
1916	Mount Sorrel, Somme, Flers-Courcelette, Ancre Heights.
1917	Arras, Vimy, Arleux, Hill 70, Ypres, Passchendaele.
1918	Arras, Amiens, Scarpe (Jigsaw Wood), Hindenburg Line, Canal du Nord (Tilloy), Pursuit to Mons. Princess Patricia of Connaught appointed Colonel-in-Chief.
1919	Return to Canada – Regiment becomes part of Permanent Active Militia – Canada's regular army.
1920—39	Stationed in Winnipeg, Manitoba and Esquimalt, British Columbia.
1924	Alliance with The Rifle Brigade (Prince Consort's Own).
1939	With Seaforth Highlanders of Canada and Edmonton Regiment forms 2nd Canadian Infantry Brigade. Moves to Britain.

1939—43	In Britain.
1943	Landing in Sicily, Leonforte, The Moro, The Gully.
1944	Hitler Line, Gothic Line, Rimini Line, San Fortunato, Fosso Munio.
1945	Granarolo, Apeldoorn – return to Canada.
1948	PPCLI becomes parachute battalion trained for arctic operations.
1950	2nd and 3rd Battalions raised for Korean War.
1950–53	Korea, Kap'yong.
1953	Formation of Regimental Depot. 2nd Battalion to Germany.
1954	3rd Battalion disbanded. The Loyal Edmonton Regiment of the Canadian Militia becomes affiliated to the Patricias and adds '(3PPCLI)' to its title.
1955	1st relieves 2nd in Germany.
1957–63	Both Battalions in Canada.
1958	Exchange of officers with The Rifle Brigade, later The Royal Green Jackets, re-instituted.
1963	1st Battalion to Germany.
1964	Golden Jubilee.
1966	2nd Battalion relieves 1st in Germany.
1968	1st Battalion to Cyprus. PPCLI Depot disbanded.
1970	3rd Battalion re-formed from 1st Battalion, Queen's Own Rifles of Canada which reverted to Militia. Proceeds Cyprus. Loyal Edmonton Regiment designation changed to '(4PPCLI)'. 2nd Battalion returns from Germany, lends aid to the civil power in Quebec Crisis. Battalion permanent stations – Calgary, Winnipeg and Esquimalt.
1971	1st Battalion – Cyprus.
1972	2nd Battalion – Cyprus.
1974	Death of Lady Patricia Ramsay who is succeeded as Colonel-in-Chief by Lady Brabourne, later Countess Mountbatten of Burma. Diamond Jubilee.
1975	3rd Battalion – Cyprus.
1975–7	1st Battalion – Allied Mobile Force (Europe).
1976	2nd Battalion – Cyprus.

1977	3rd Battalion – Cyprus.
1978	Alliance with Royal Australian Regiment. 1st Battalion – Cyprus.
1980	3rd Battalion – Cyprus.
1981	PPCLI Battle School formed at Camp Wainwright, Alberta.
1982	2nd Battalion – Cyprus.
1984	1st Battalion – Cyprus. 2nd Battalion to Germany in July.

Appendix II

THE COLOURS

In August, 1914, Princess Patricia of Connaught presented the Regiment with a 'camp colour' which she had designed and embroidered herself. After being carried in every action of the First World War, it was consecrated in Belgium as the Regimental Colour in 1919.

On 21 February of that year, at Liphook, Surrey, when the Regiment paraded to say farewell to their Colonel-in-Chief, she decorated the Colour with a Wreath of Laurel – the only time in the history of the armies of the British Commonwealth that such an award has been made.

In 1922, the original Colour was laid away as the Patricias' most treasured possession. The Governor-General, Viscount Byng of Vimy, presented the Regiment with a replica and with a silk Union Flag to be used as a King's Colour.

It was not until 1934 that Princess Patricia's Canadian Light Infantry received King's and Regimental Colours whose design was officially approved by the College of Heralds. They were carried by the 1st Battalion until July 1959.

In September, 1953, at Calgary, the Colonel-in-Chief gave Colours to her 2nd Battalion and in July, 1959, the Queen presented new ones to the 1st Battalion at Victoria, BC.

When the 2nd Battalion's Colours were replaced in 1969 and when Lady Brabourne presented new ones to the 1st on 8 May, 1977, the Union Flag was supplanted as the Queen's Colour by the National Flag of Canada. During the Jubilee celebrations of 1964, Lady Patricia Ramsay gave both the 1st and 2nd Battalions replicas of the Wreath of Laurel to carry on their Regimental Colours. The original Wreath now rests with the Patricias' first Colour in the Regimental museum in Calgary. When in 1971, the 3rd Battalion received their first Colours from the Governor-General, the Honourable Roland Michener, a replica of the Wreath was presented to them by Major-General C. B. Ware on behalf of the Colonel-in-Chief.

Except for the designation 'I', 'II' and 'III' the Colours of the three Battalions are identical. The 2nd wears the Kap'yong streamer, symbol of the United States Presidential Citation on the pike of its Regimental Colour. On it are emblazoned twenty-two of the Regiment's battle honours.

The background of the Regimental Colour is unique in that it, and the regimental facings, are of French grey. This was the colour of the patch of the 3rd Canadian Division in which the Regiment served during most of the First World War. In a sense it commemorates the Patricias' baptism of fire during the relief of a unit of the French Army in January, 1915.

Appendix III

BATTLE HONOURS

In the following list of Battle Honours won by the Regiment, those emblazoned on the Colours are shown in capital letters.

First World War

YPRES, 1915, 17
FREZENBERG
MOUNT SORREL
FLERS-COURCELETTE
VIMY, 1917
PASSCHENDAELE
AMIENS
SCARPE, 1918
PURSUIT TO MONS
FRANCE AND FLANDERS, 1914–18

Bellewaarde
Somme, 1916
Ancre Heights
Arras, 1917, 18
Arleux
Hill 70
Hindenburg Line
Canal du Nord

Second World War

LANDING IN SICILY
LEONFORTE
THE MORO
THE GULLY
HITLER LINE
GOTHIC LINE
RIMINI LINE
SAN FORTUNATO
FOSSO MUNIO
NORTH-WEST EUROPE, 1945

Agira
Sicily, 1943
Liri Valley
Savio Bridgehead
Naviglio Canal
Granarolo
Italy, 1943–45
Apeldoorn

Korea

KAP'YONG
KOREA, 1950–53

Appendix IV

REGIMENTAL MARCHES and BUGLE CALL

A child of the First World War, the Regiment chose a medley of songs they had sung in France – 'Has Anyone Seen the Colonel', 'Mademoiselle from Armentières' and 'Tipperary' as the Regimental March. After the Second World War, the Regiment selected as its Slow March, 'Lili Marlene', a tune sung with various words* as much by the Canadians as their enemies.

Each battalion has a march which is played when necessary to distinguish it on parade. That for the 1st Battalion is 'The Maple Leaf', the 2nd is 'March Winnipeg' and the 3rd 'Imperial Echoes'. The Regimental March of The Loyal Edmonton Regiment (4 PPCLI) is 'Bonnie Dundee'.

The soldier takes some of his orders from the bugle. Those which apply to Princess Patricia's Canadian Light Infantry are preceded by the 'Regimental Call'.

* A proportion of each Canadian infantry battalion was usually 'Left Out of Battle' (LOB) so that it could be quickly re-formed if it met with disaster, hence the LOB SONG of which the following are two verses:

> When you meet the Wehrmacht across the next canal,
> This is the time I wish you well, Old Pal,
> When you go into that attack,
> Just think of me, I'm ten miles back,
> For I am LOB – for I am LOB.

When you hear the Tigers grinding by your slit,
Makes you start to wonder if it's time to quit,
Just think of me in gay Paree,
With some French wench upon my knee.
For I am LOB – for I am LOB.

Appendix V

COLONELS and COMMANDING OFFICERS

From its formation in 1914, the Regiment regarded Princess Patricia of Connaught as its Colonel-in-Chief although she was not formally appointed to that position by King George V until 22 February, 1918. In 1920, Lieutenant-Colonel Hamilton Gault was made the Honorary Lieutenant-Colonel of the Regiment. In 1948, he became its first Honorary Colonel and, in 1958, its first Colonel of the Regiment.

Listed below are the Colonels-in-Chief, Colonels of the Regiment and Commanding Officers of Battalions with the year of their appointment.

Colonels-in-Chief

Princess Patricia of Connaught	
(after marriage, Lady Patricia Ramsay, CI, CD)	1918
The Rt Hon The Countess Mountbatten of	
Burma, CD, JP, DL (until her succession to	
that title, Lady Brabourne)	1974

Colonels of the Regiment

Brig A. H. Gault, DSO, ED, CD	1958
Maj-Gen C. B. Ware, DSO, CD	1959
Maj-Gen G. G. Brown, OStJ, CD	1977
Col W. B. S. Sutherland, CD	1983

Commanding Officers

Lieutenant-Colonels:		Lieutenant-Colonels:	
F. D. Farquhar, DSO	1914	R. A. Lindsay, ED	1941
H. C. Buller, DSO	1915 & 16	C. B. Ware, DSO, CD	1943 & 46
R. T. Pelly, DSO	1915 & 16	D. H. Rosser	1944
A. S. A. M. Adamson, DSO	1916	R. P. Clark, DSO	1944
C. J. T. Stewart, DSO	1918	*Major:*	
A. G. Pearson, MC, DCM	1918	P. D. Crofton	1945
A. H. Gault, DSO	1918	*Lieutenant-Colonel:*	
C. R. E. Willets, DSO, ADC	1920	P. W. Strickland, DSO, ED	1945
M. R. Ten Broeke, MC	1927	*Major:*	
H. W. Niven, DSO, MC	1932	W. H. V. Matthews, MC	1945
W. G. Colquhoun, MC	1937	*Lieutenant-Colonels:*	
J. N. Edgar, MC	1940	N. M. Gemmell, DSO	1947
R. F. L. Keller	1941	D. C. Cameron, DSO, ED	1948
C. Vokes	1941		

First Battalion

D. C. Cameron, DSO, ED	1950	A. M. Potts, CD	1968
N. G. Wilson-Smith,		W. E. J. Hutchinson, CD	1969
DSO, MBE	1950	C. W. Hewson, CD	1971
J. R. Cameron, OBE	1952	J. L. Sharpe, CD	1973
T. de Faye, MBE	1955	K. R. Foster, CD	1975
J. C. Allan, DSO, MBE, CD	1959	L. W. MacKenzie, CD	1977
R. F. Bruce, MBE, CD	1961	G. M. Reay, MBE, CD	1979
G. G. Brown, CD	1962	R. R. Crabbe, CD	1981
H. Moncrief, CD	1965	J. S. H. Kempling, CD	1983

Second Battalion

J. R. Stone, DSO, MC	1950	A. J. G. D. de Chastelain, CD	1971
S. C. Waters, CD	1953	J. H. Allan, CD	1972
V. R. Schjelderup, DSO, MC, CD	1957	R. I. Stewart, CD	1974
C. J. A. Hamilton, MBE, CD	1960	J. E. L. Gollner, CD	1976
E. M. K. MacGregor, MC, CD	1962	W. H. Minnis, CD	1978
L. W. Basham, CD	1965	J. S. Bremner, CD	1980
R. S. Peacock, CD	1967	B. W. Ashton, CD	1982
C. B. Snider, MC, CD	1969	I. H. Gray, CD	1984

Third Battalion

G. C. Corbould, DSO, ED	1950	R. L. Cowling, CD	1973
H. F. Wood, CD	1951	H. G. Leitch, CD	1975
M. F. MacLachlan, OBE, MC, CD	1953–4	G. K. Courbould, CD	1977
T. M. C. Marsaw, CD	1970	W. B. Vernon, CD	1979
P. A. Roy, CD	1971	C. R. Wellwood, CD	1981
		M. H. McMurray, CD	1983